AF479963

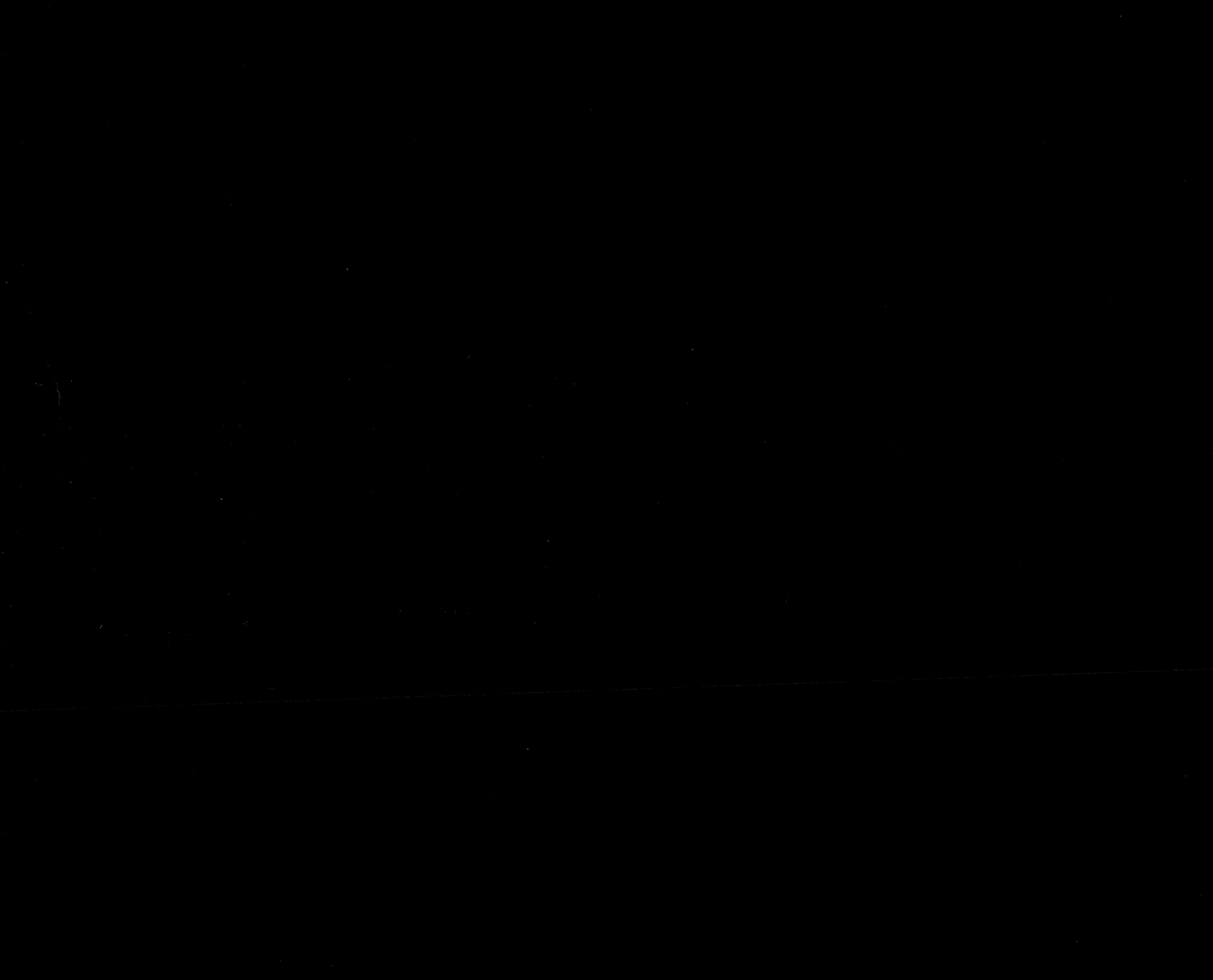

Seattle Safari

As I wandered around the vibrant habitats of the Seattle Zoo, my camera allowed me to peer into the fascinating world of its residents. Whether it was the swift elegance of cheetahs racing through the savannah or the peaceful grandeur of towering elephants, every snapshot captured the natural beauty and wild essence of the animal kingdom. Playful monkeys swung from branch to branch, their inquisitive eyes mirroring the intricate web of life in the jungle. Through my lens, I aimed to not only photograph their physical features but also to convey the essence of their individual personalities, each picture narrating a distinct tale of strength, curiosity, and the timeless connection shared by all creatures, big and small.

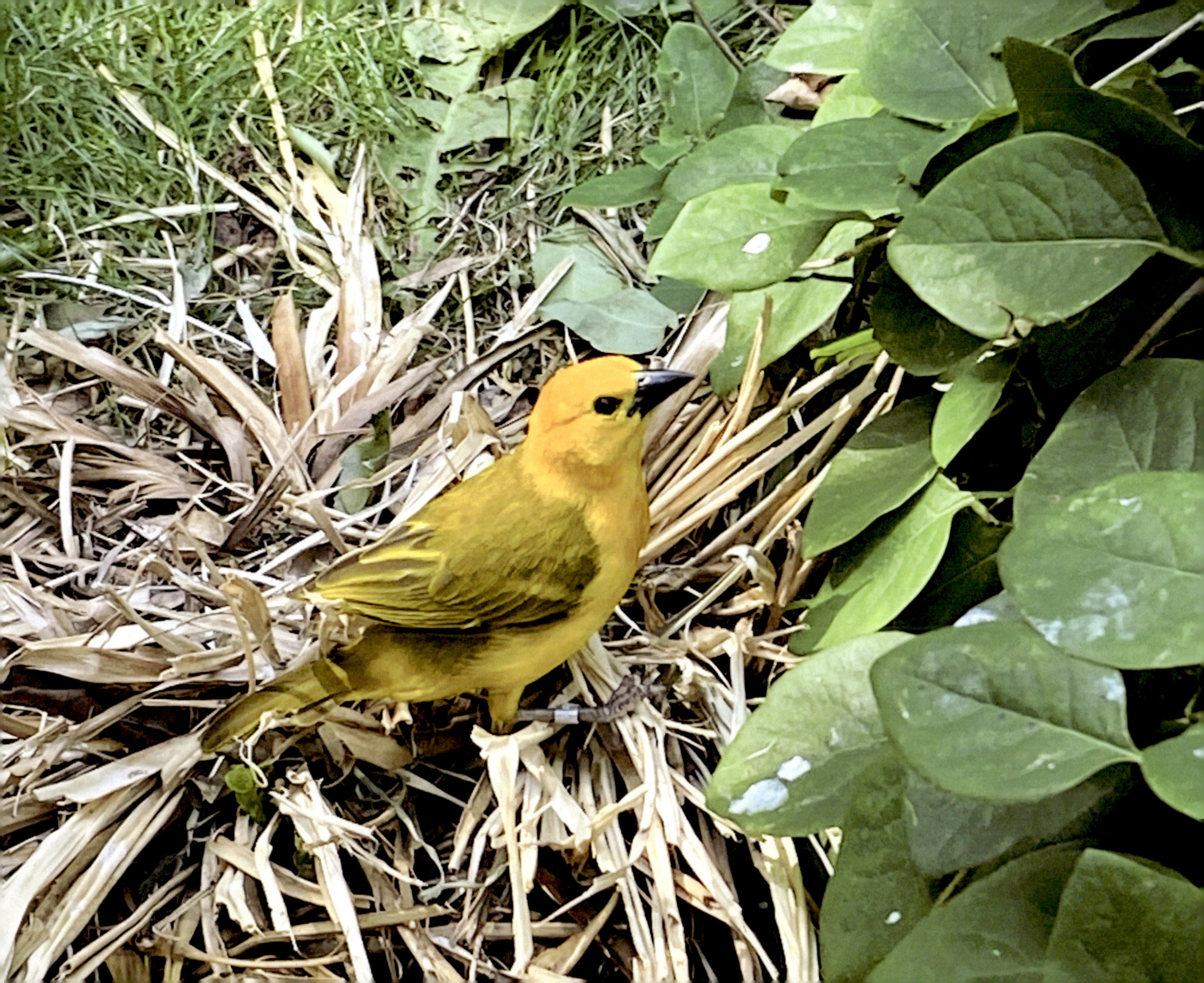

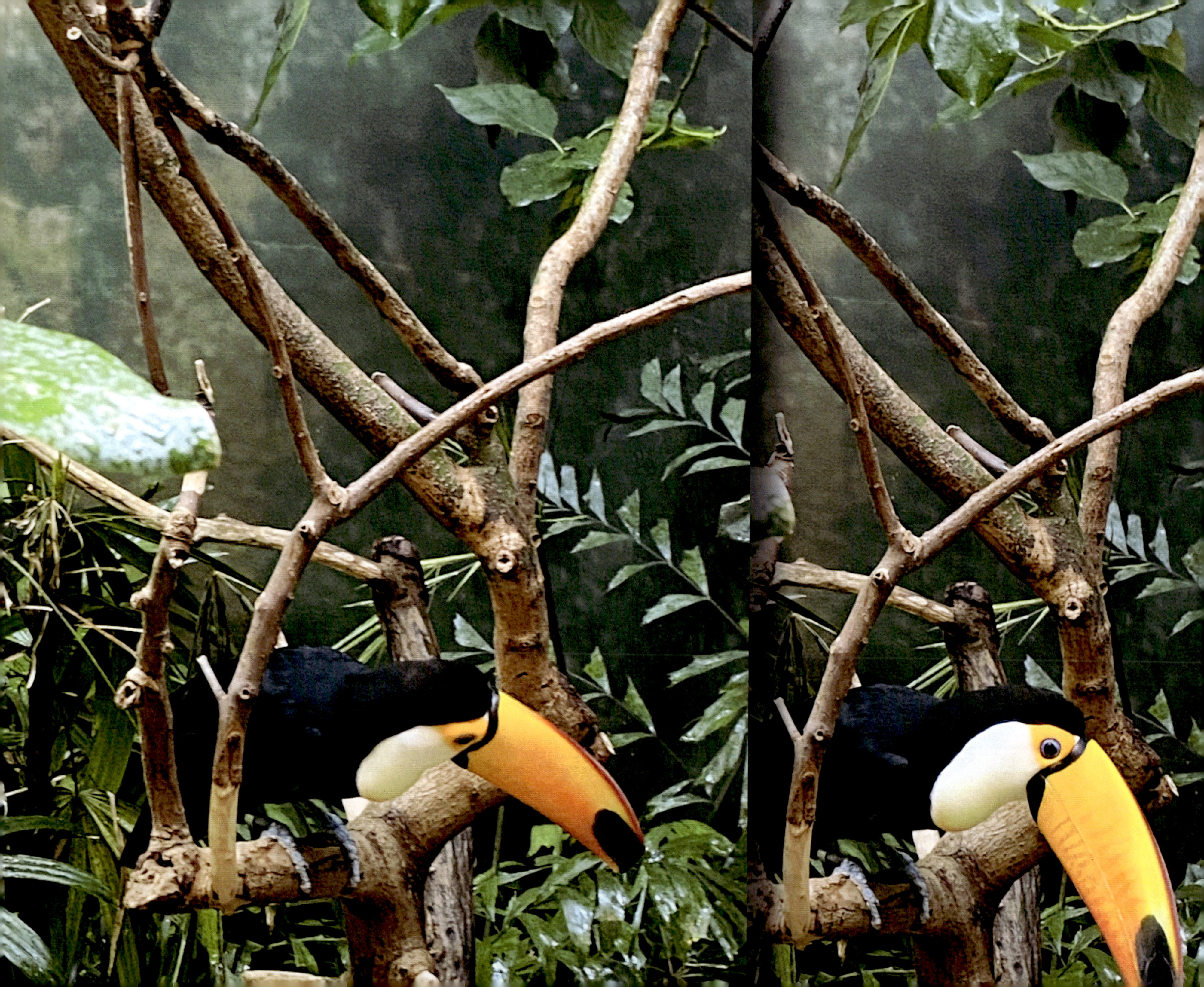

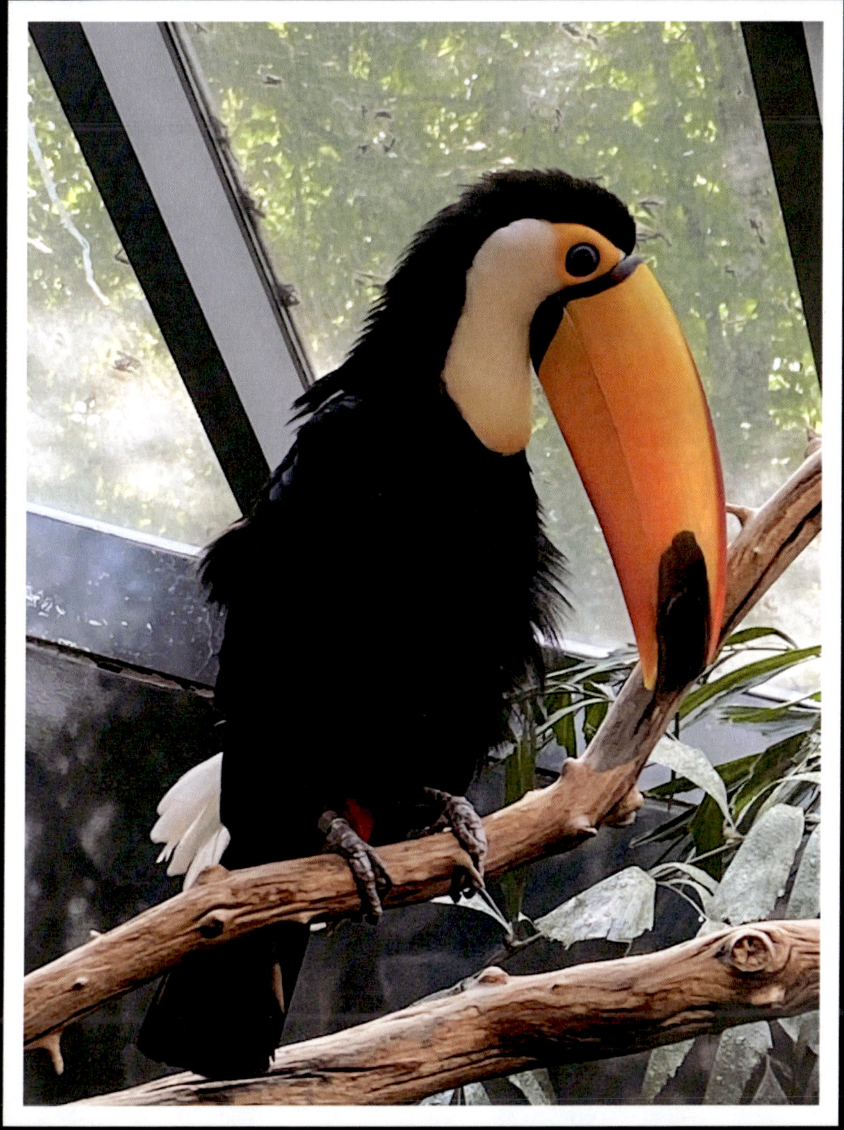

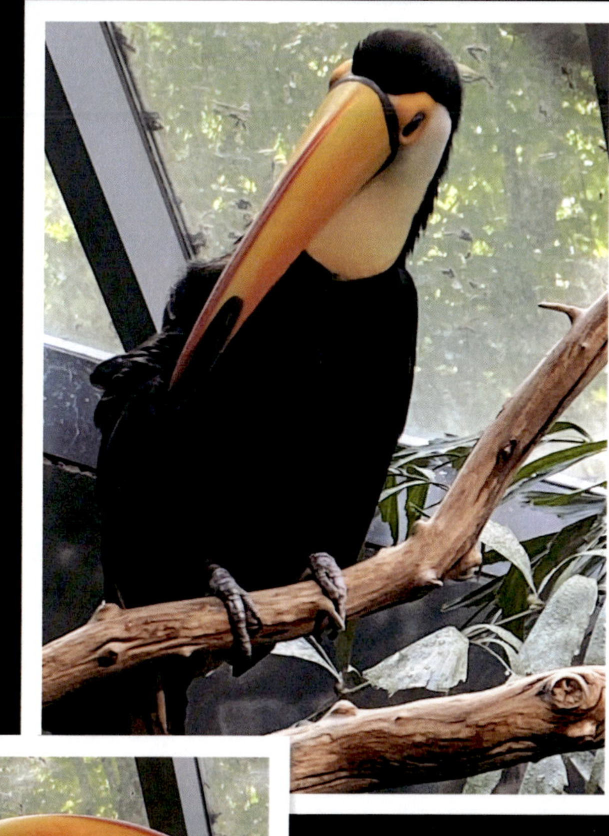

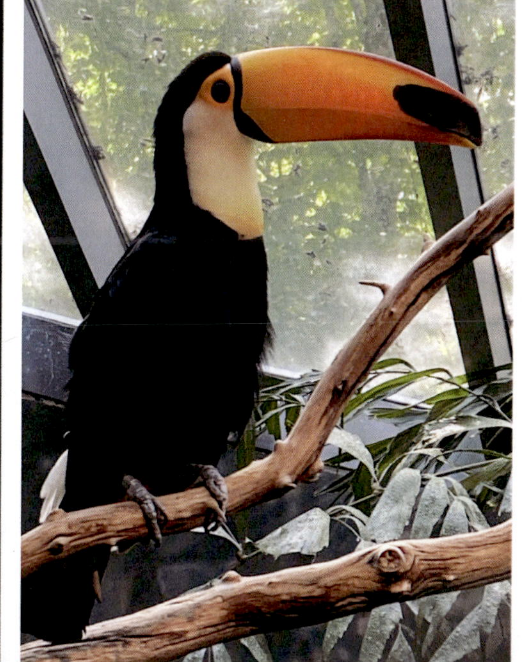

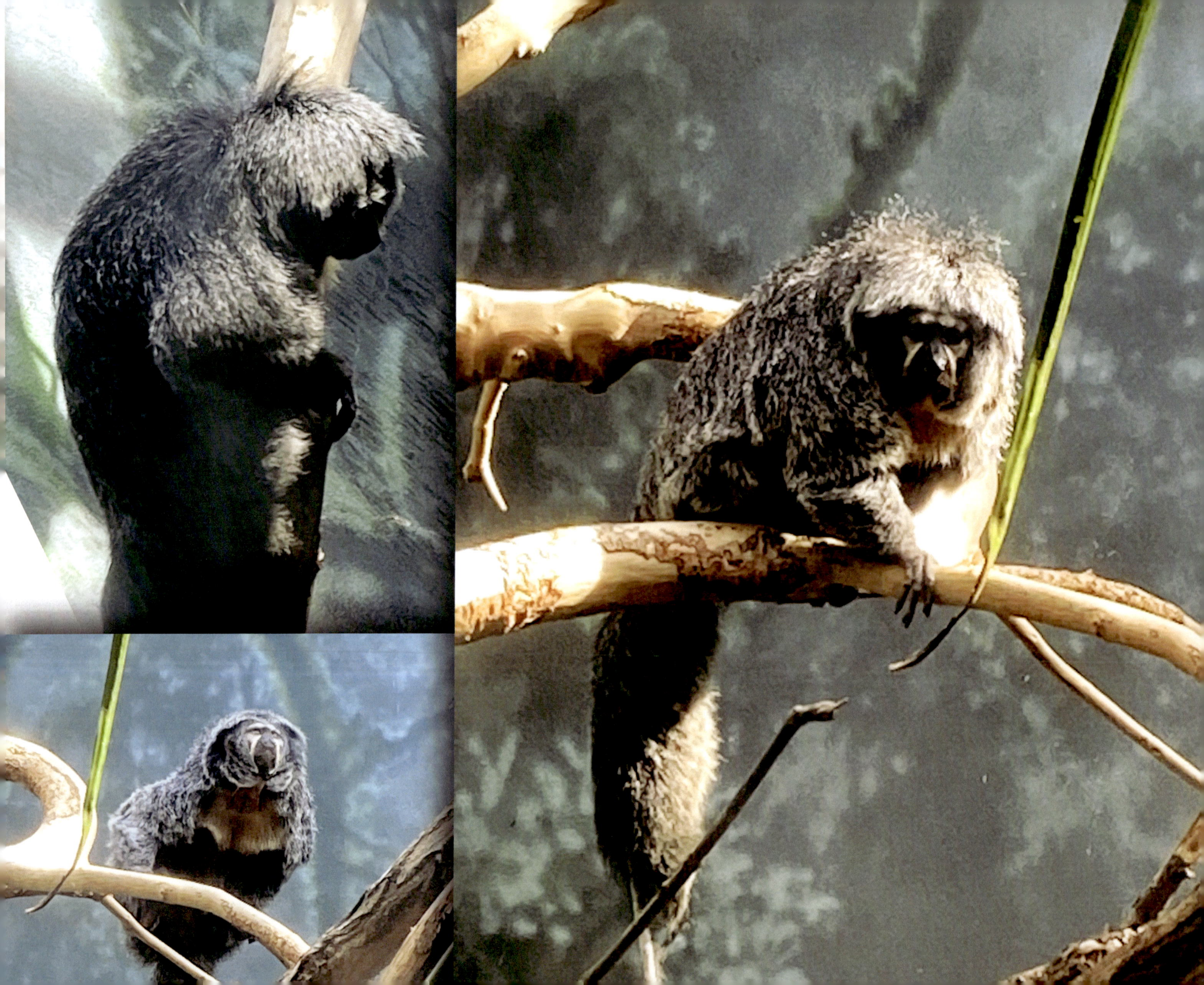

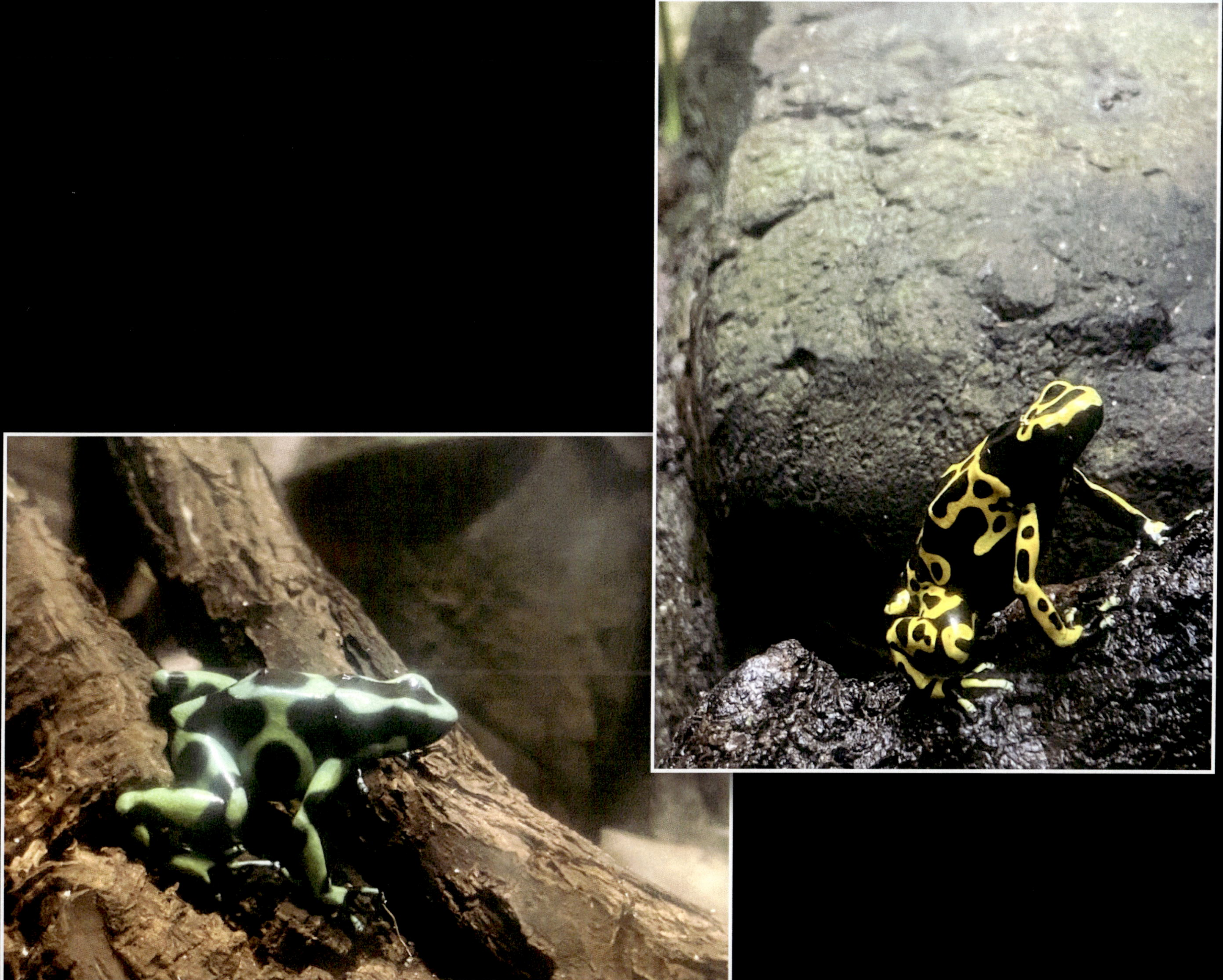

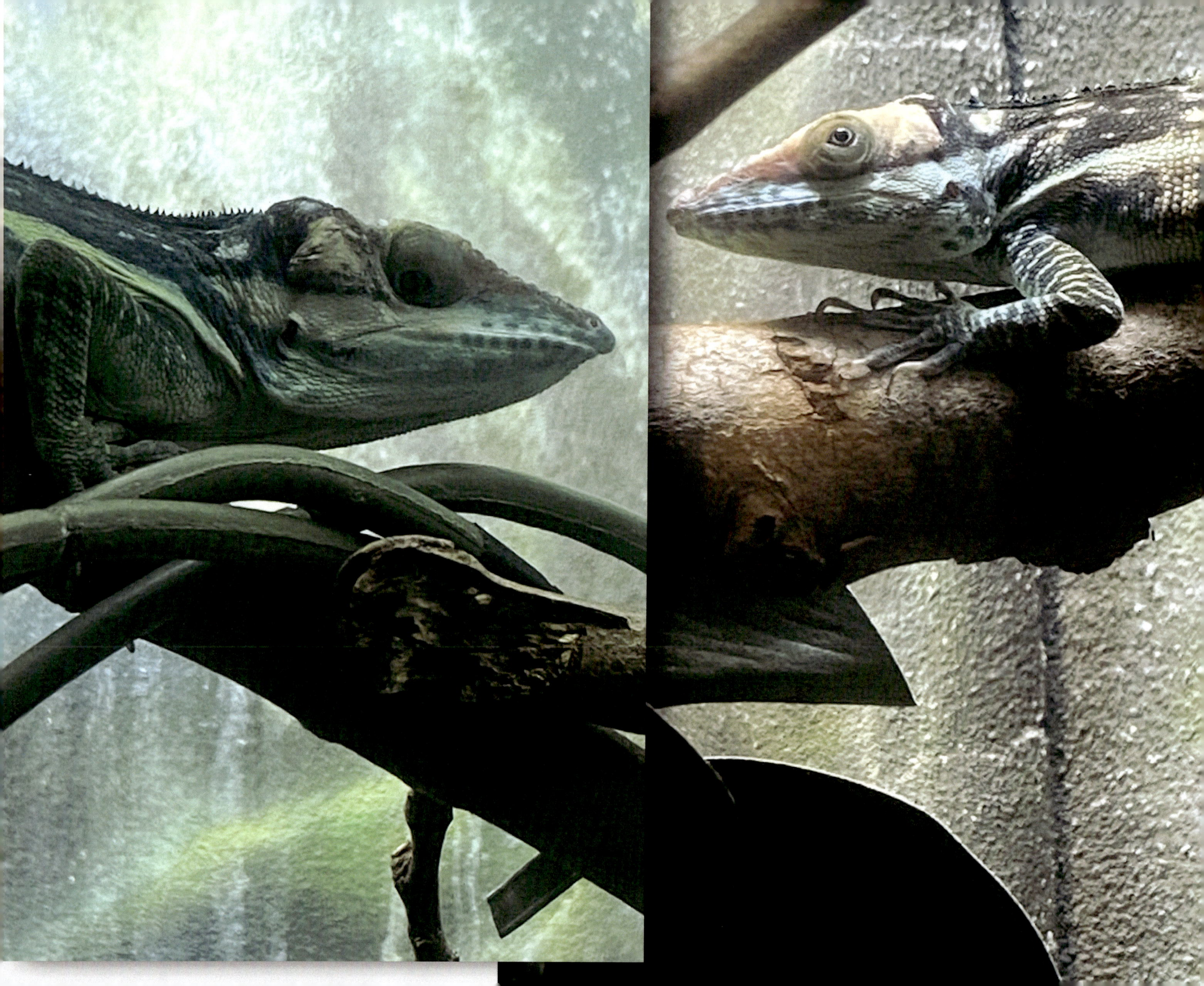

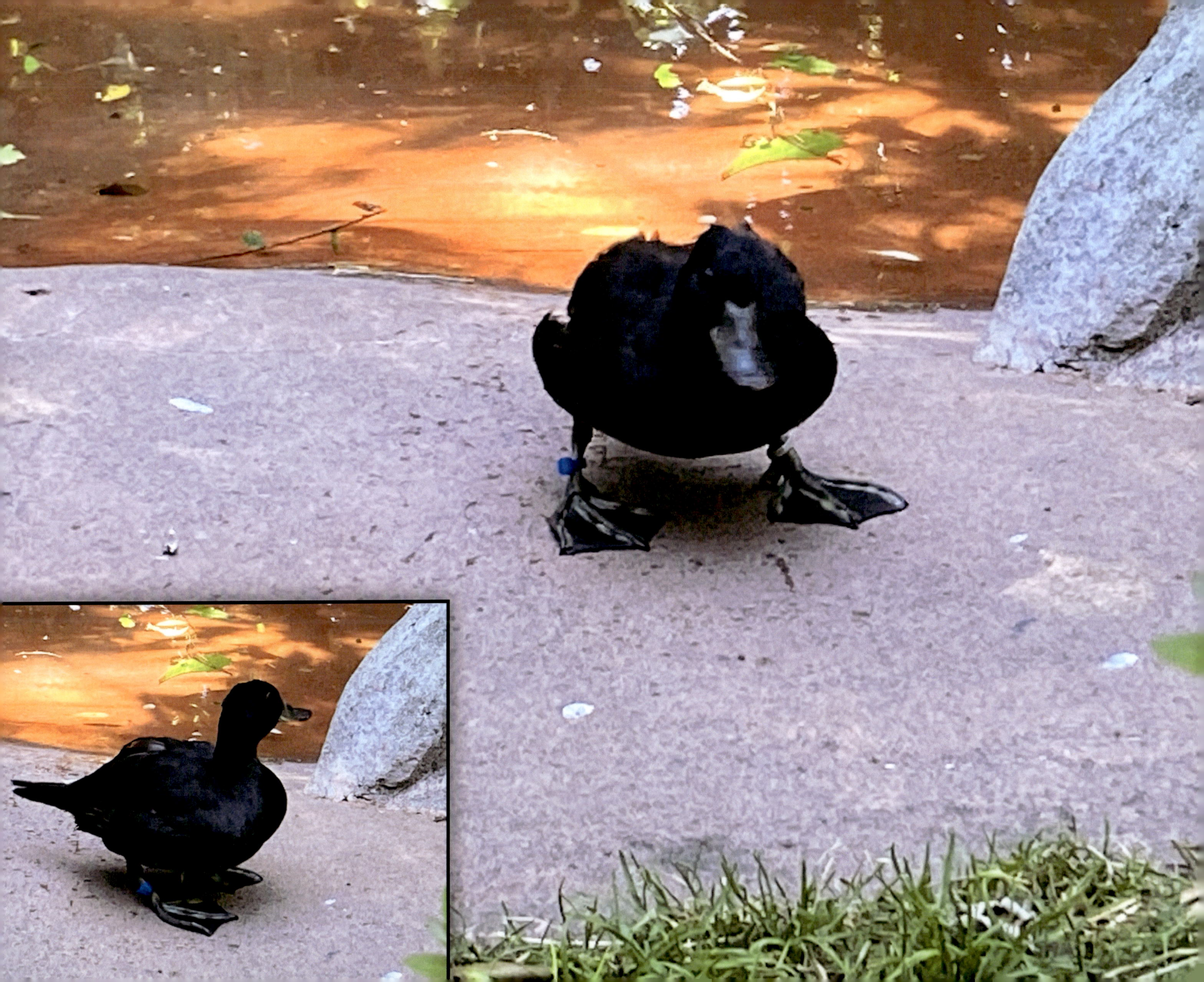

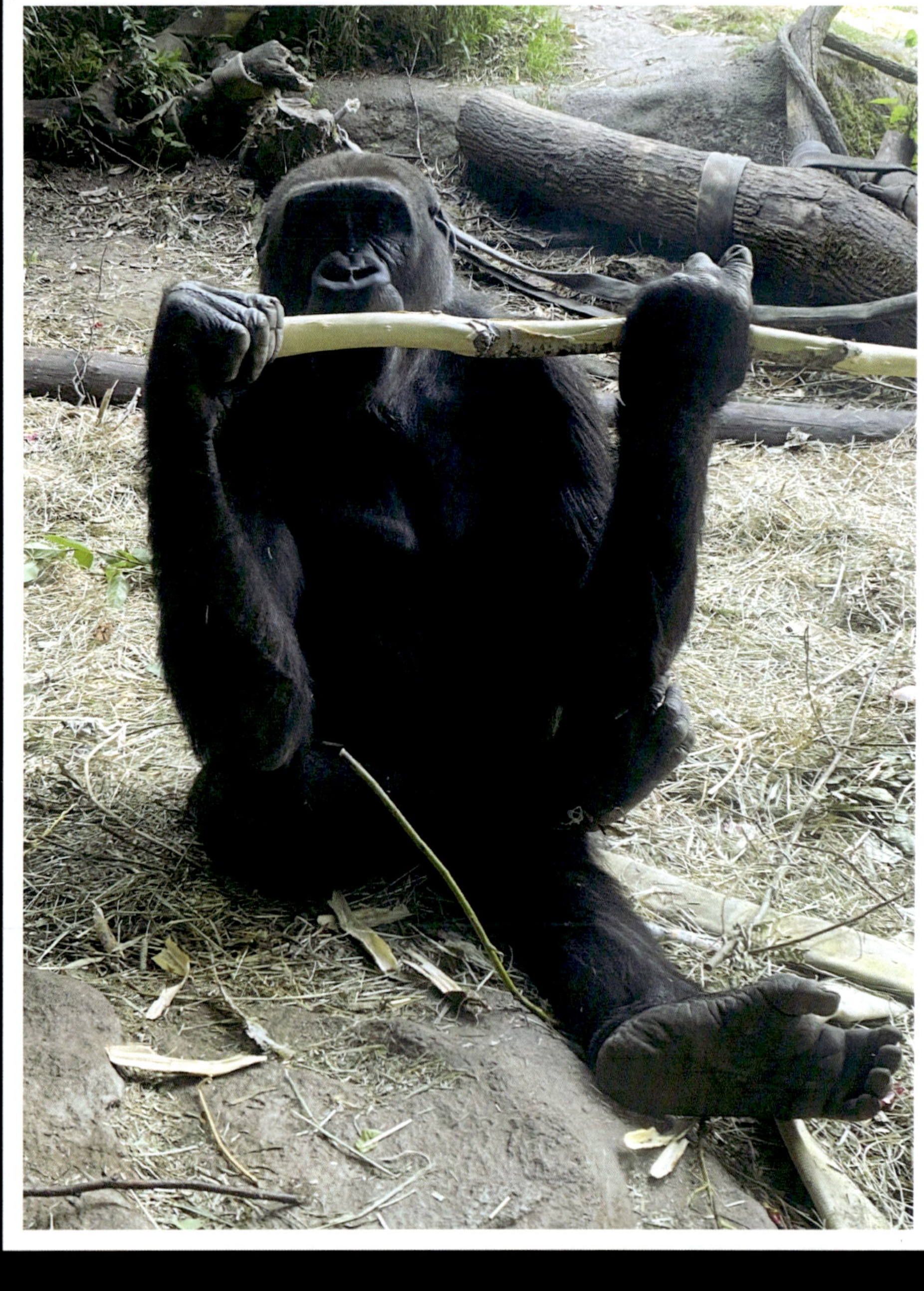

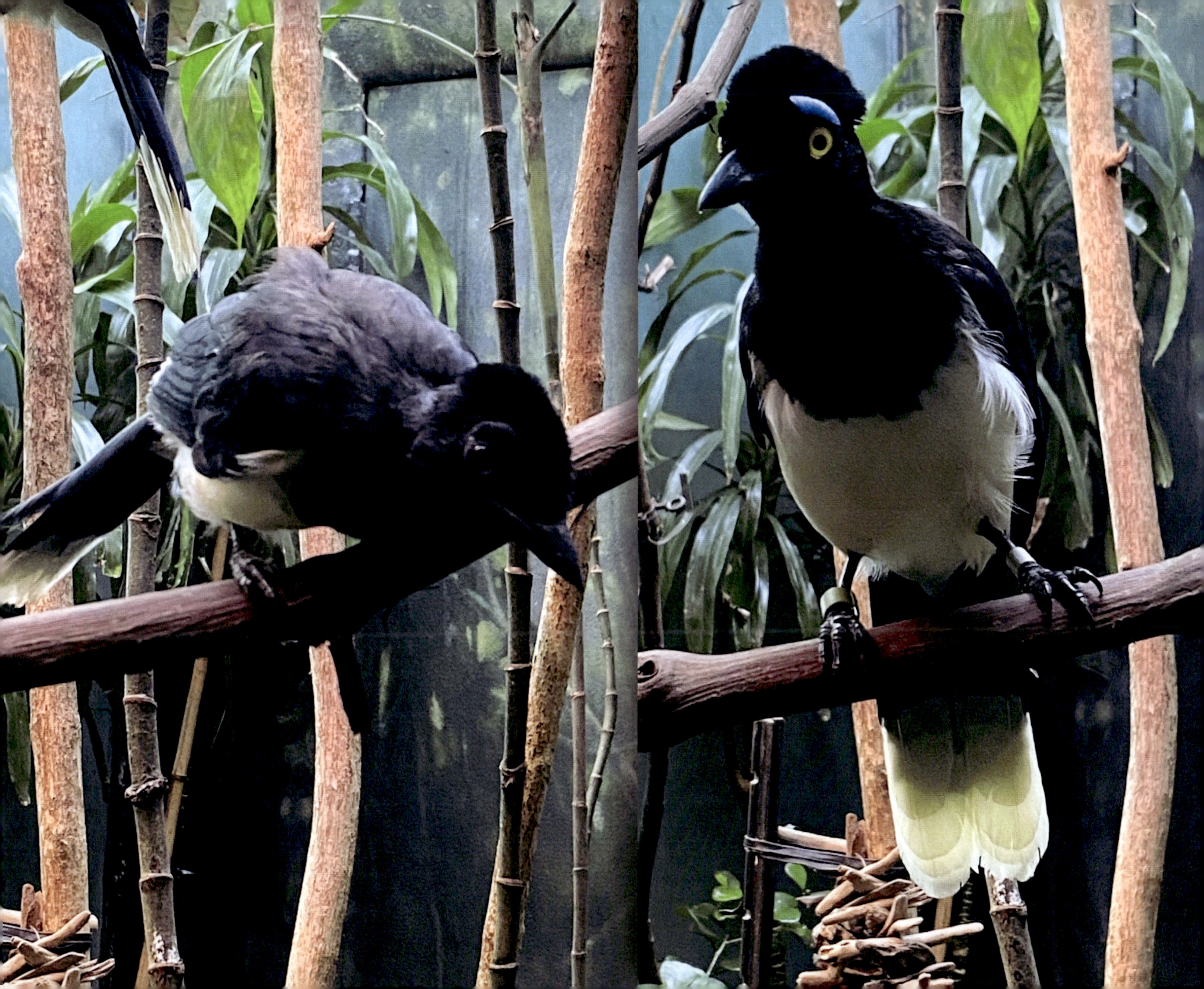

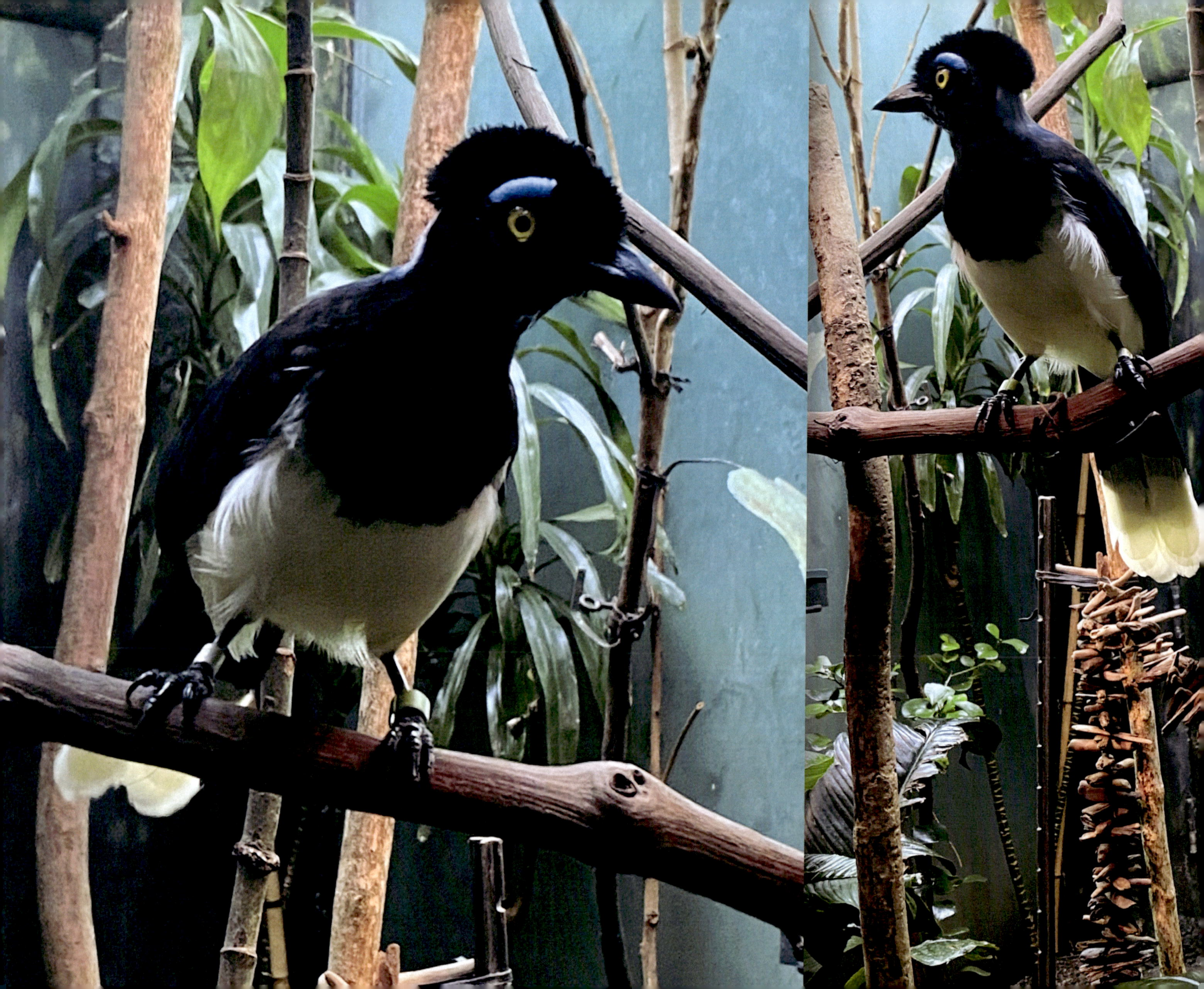

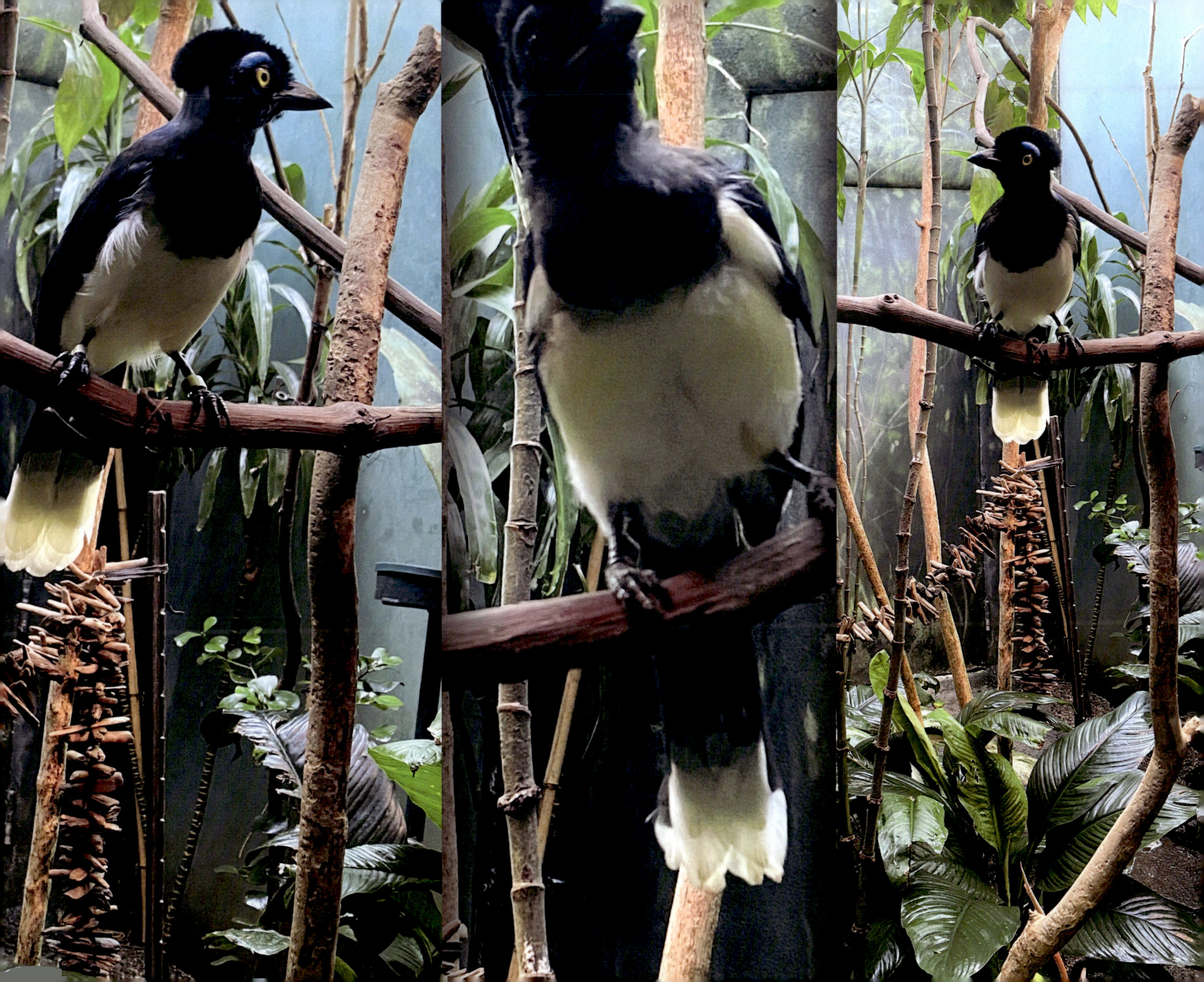

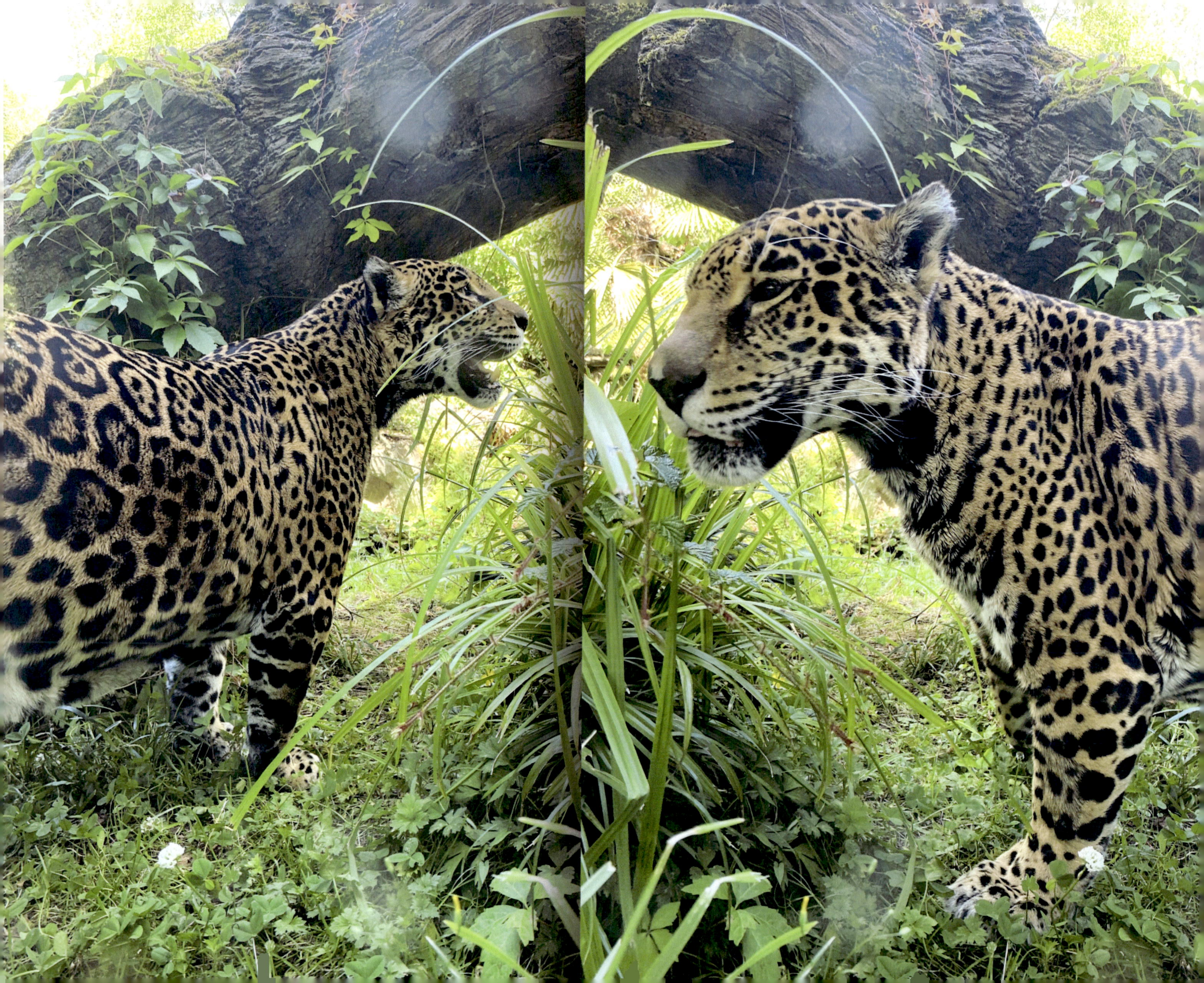

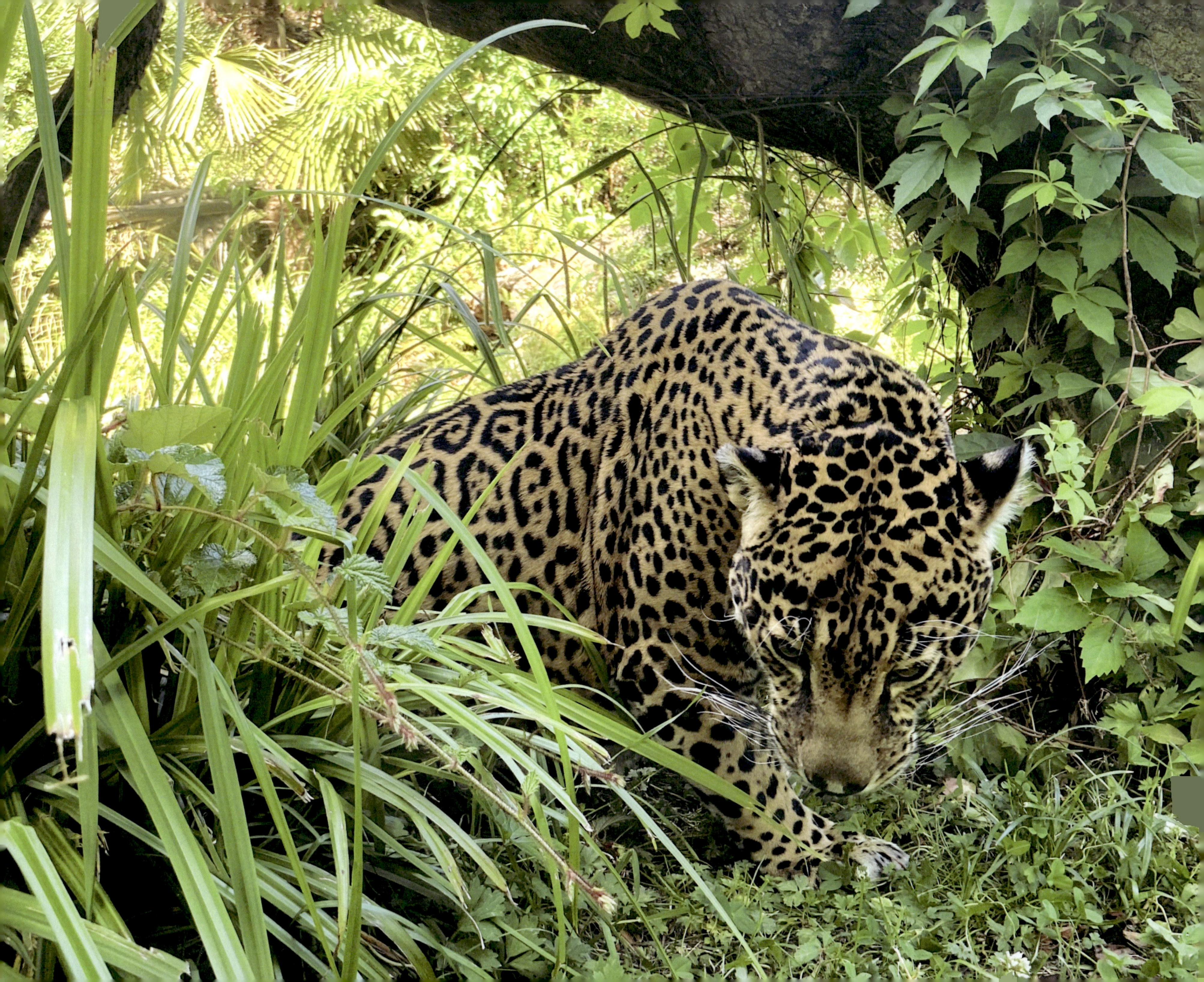

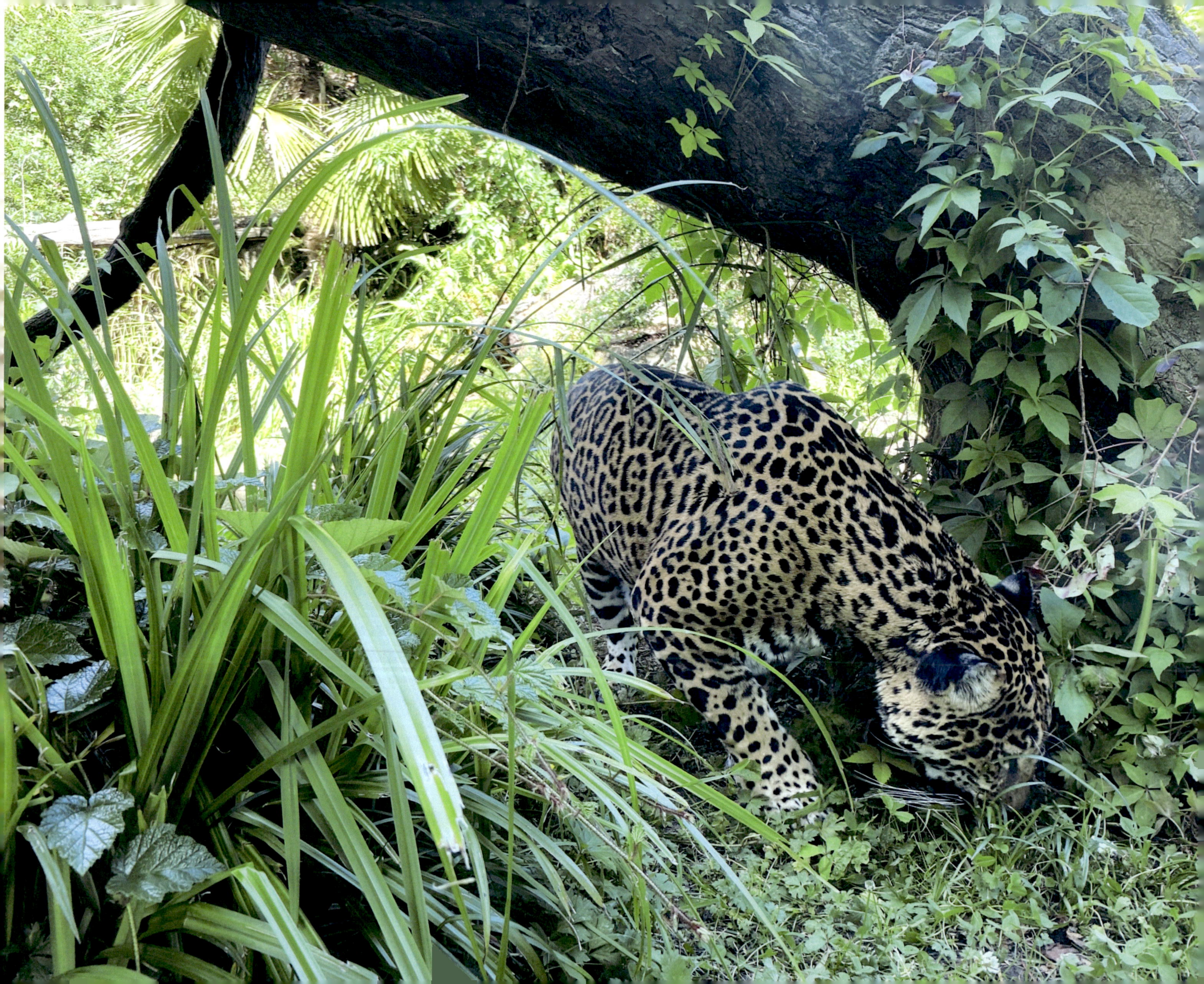

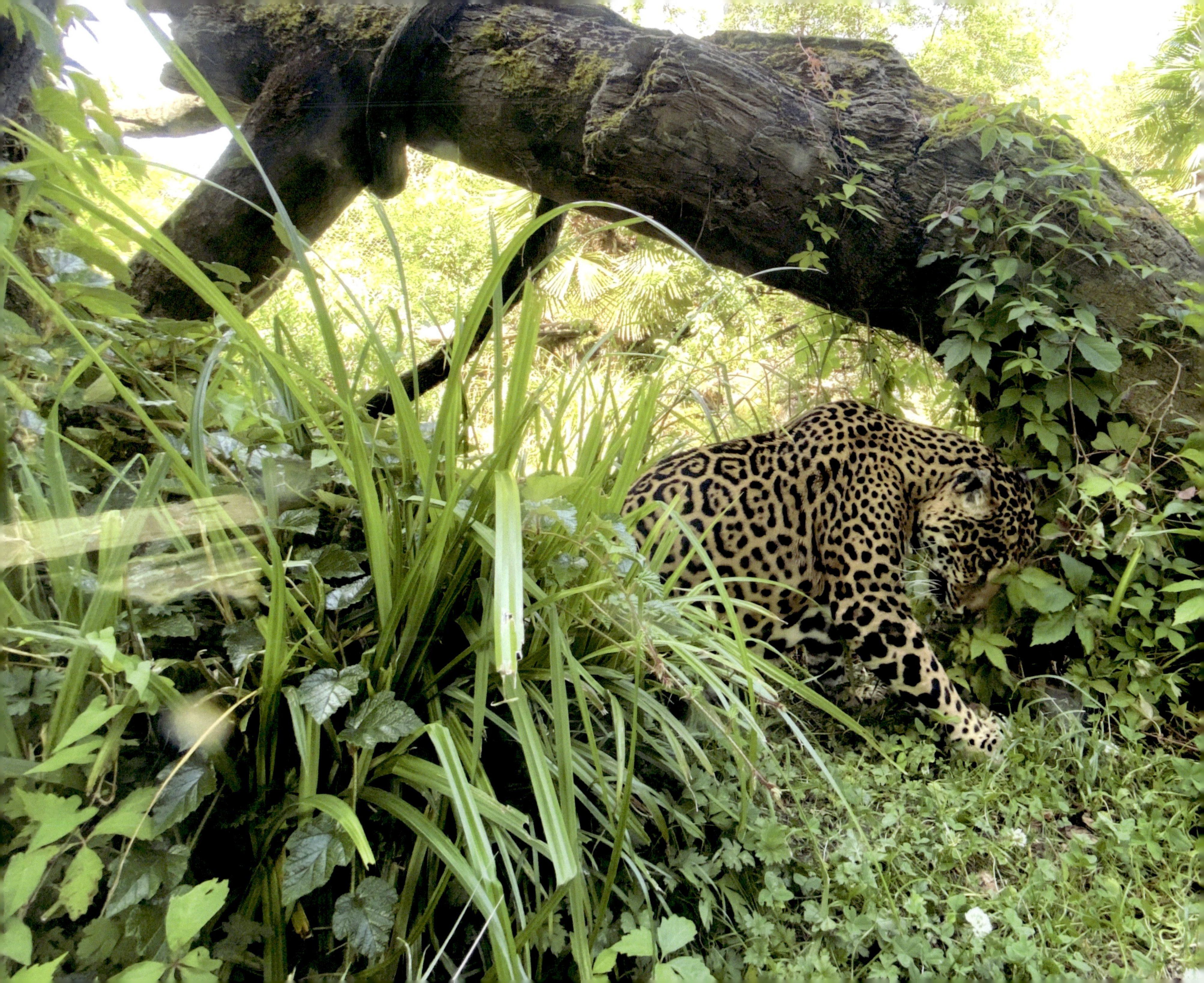

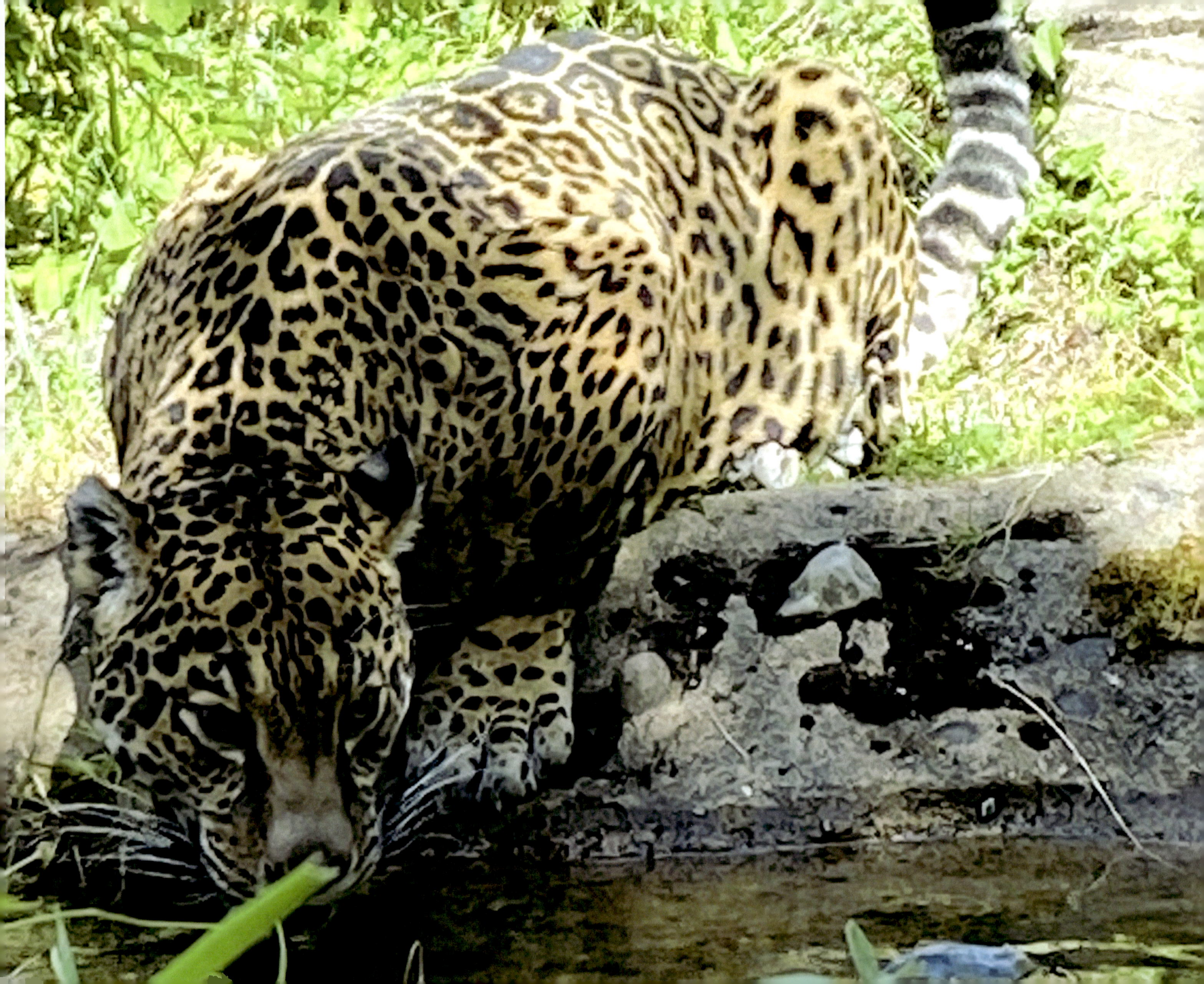

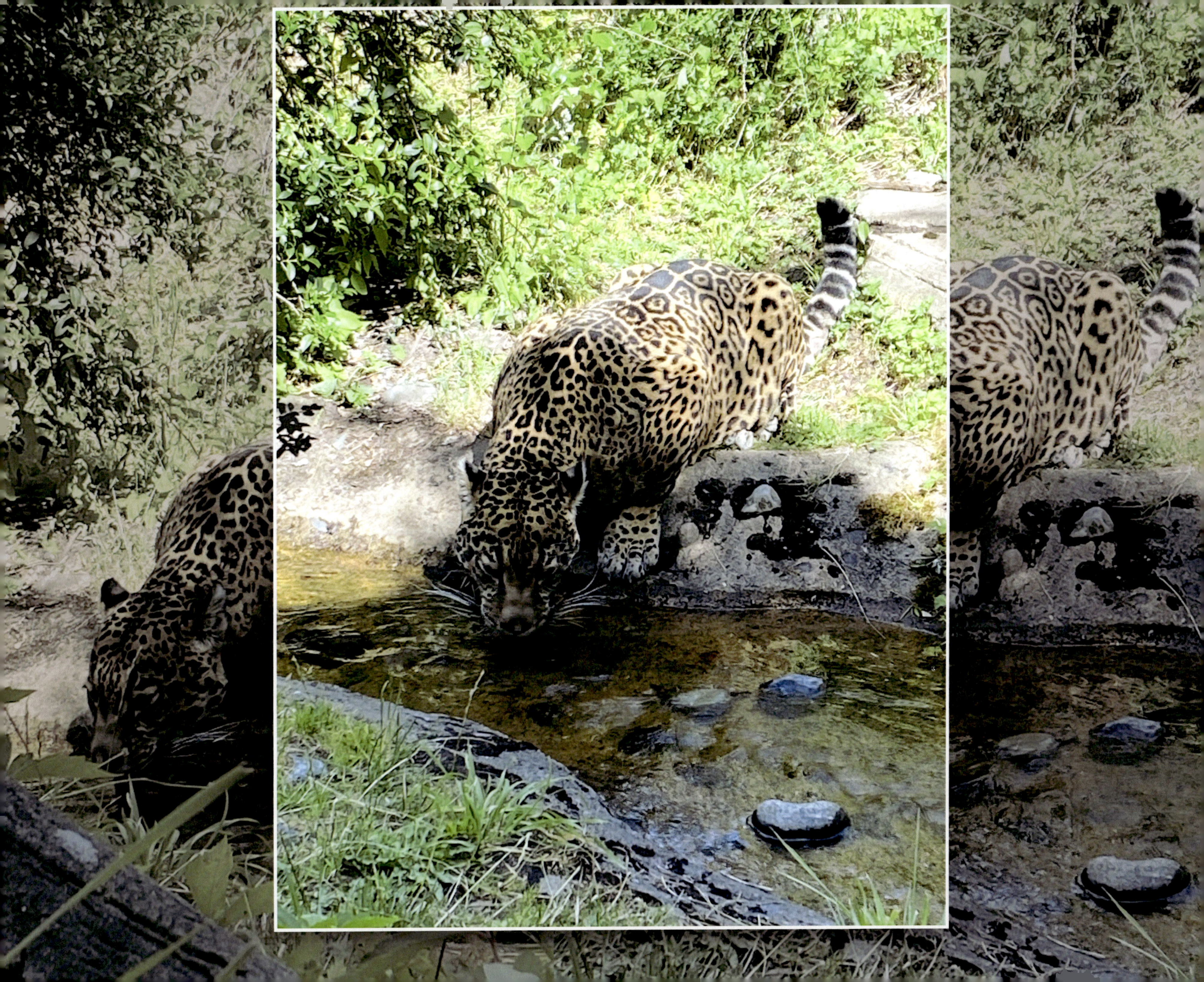

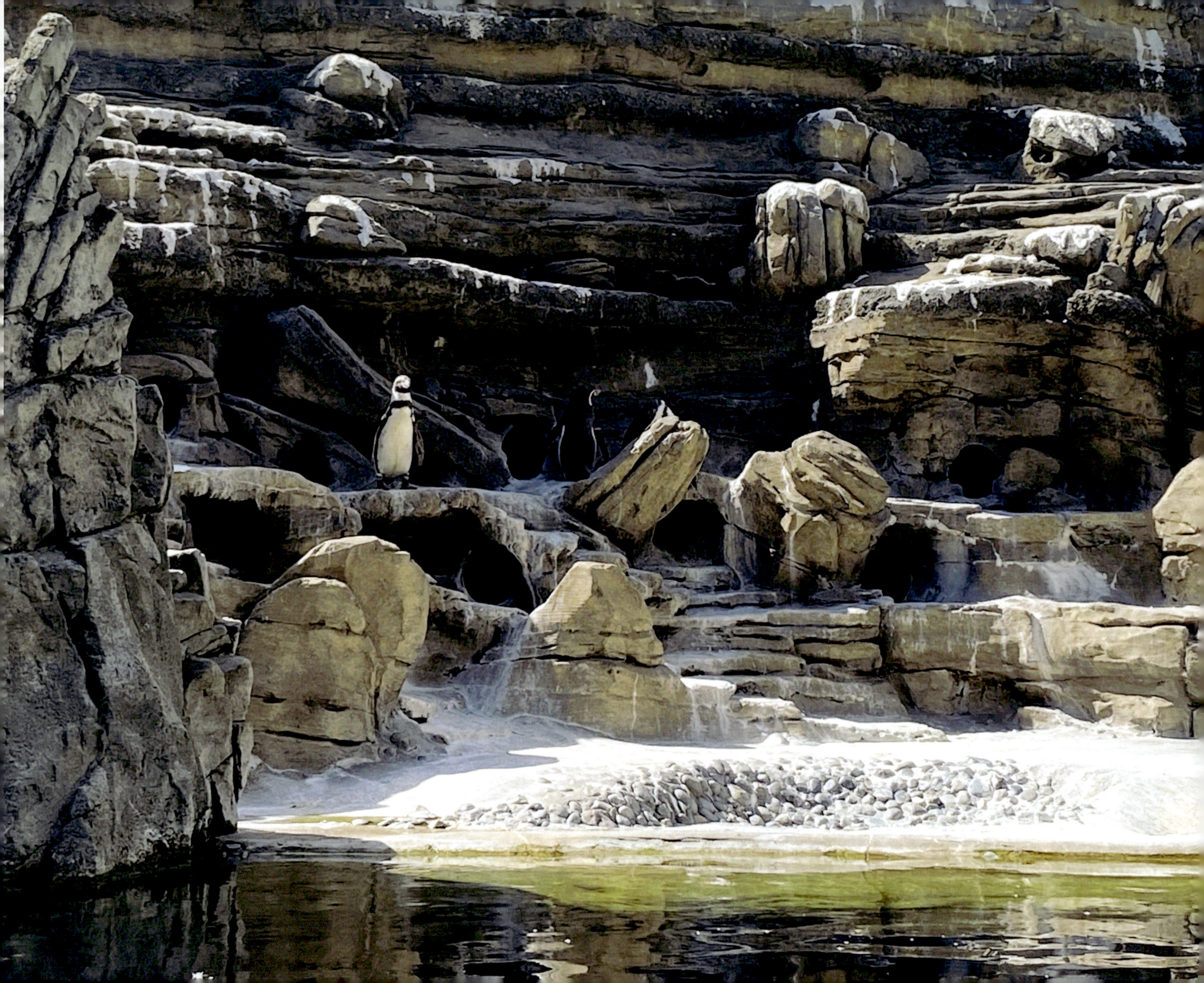

Seattle Skyline

As I delved into Seattle's architectural tapestry, I was completely engrossed in a mesmerizing blend of design. It was a perfect symphony where the past and present harmoniously coexisted. The city's rich history intertwined with modern innovation, and traditional charm gracefully danced with contemporary elements. Each photograph I took encapsulated the very essence of this vibrant city, telling a story of towering skyscrapers that seemed to touch the sky, while also capturing the whispers of bygone days in the quaint historical buildings. From the sleek and modern structures to the intricate facades of century-old landmarks, my camera lens captured the diverse personality of Seattle's urban landscape. It was an invitation for viewers to embark on a journey through time and space, all within the confines of a single frame.

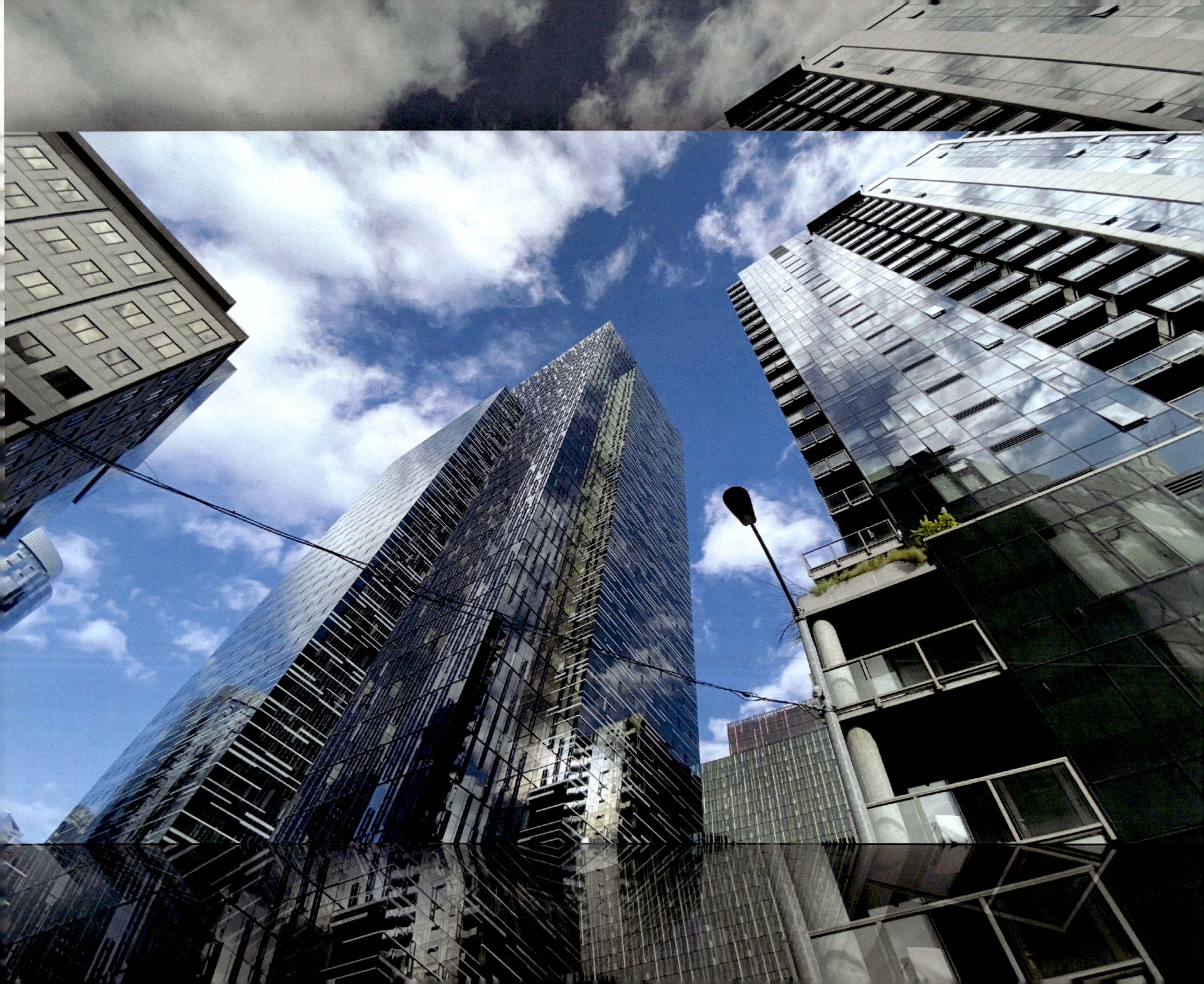

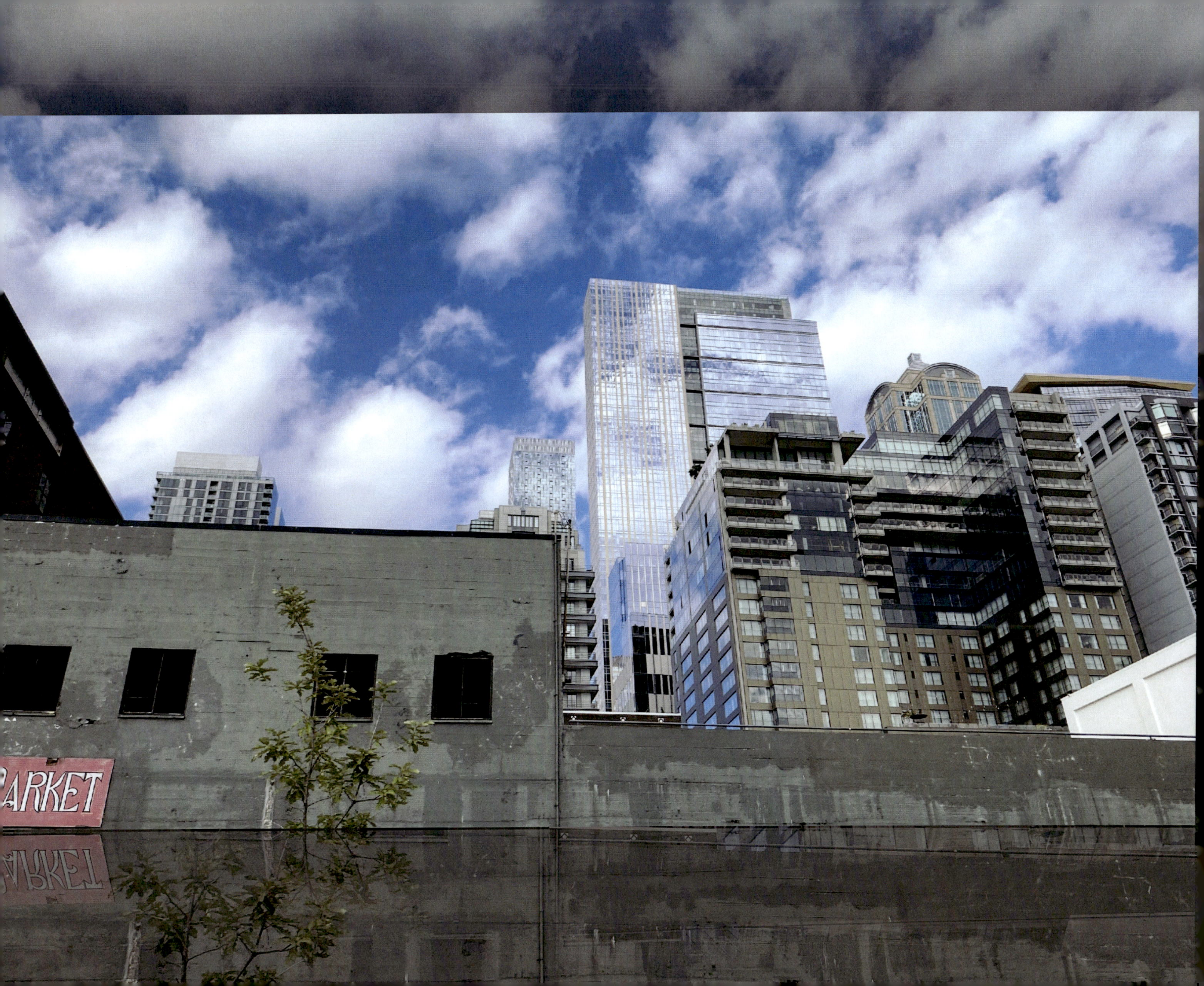
ARKET

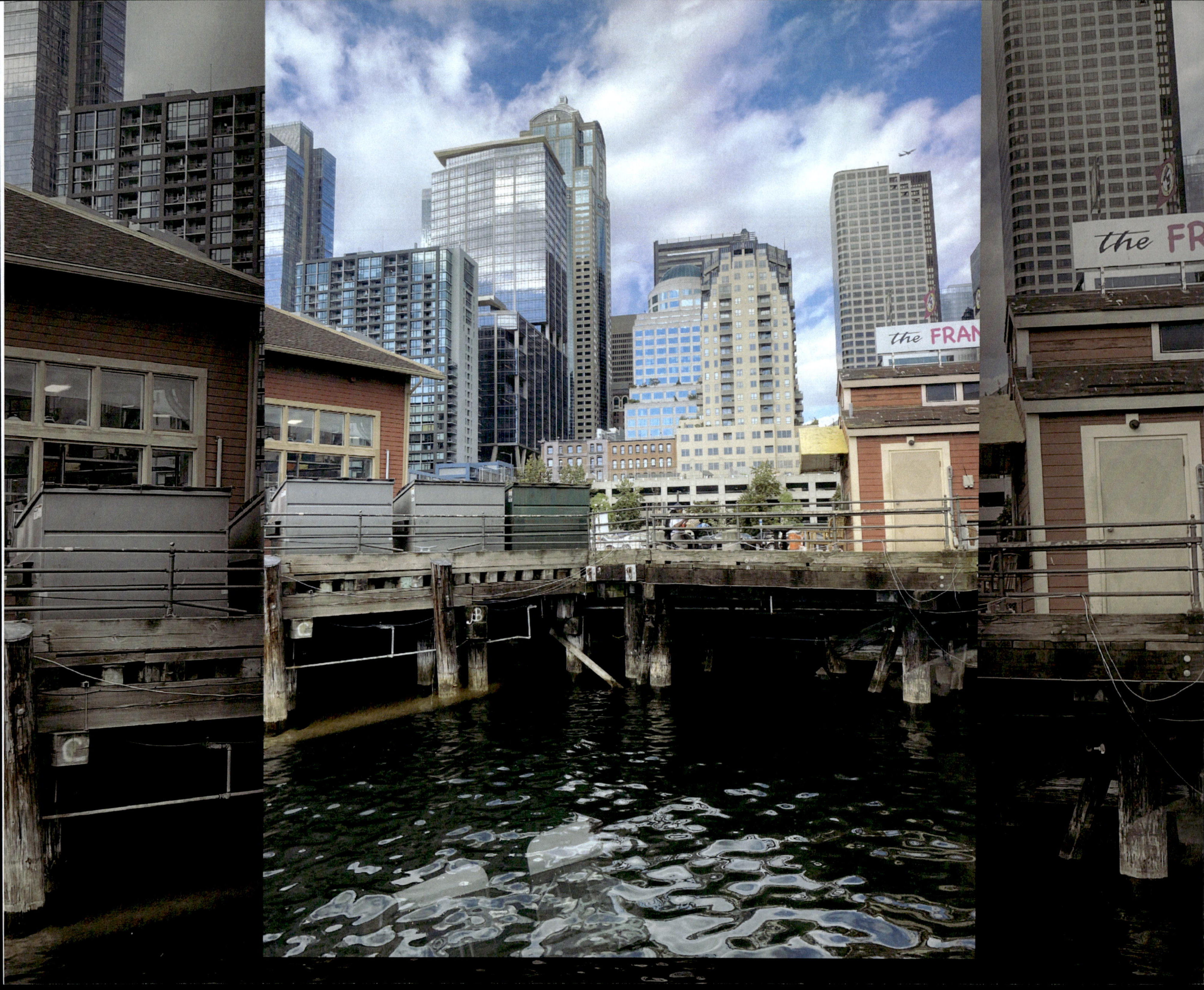
the FRAN

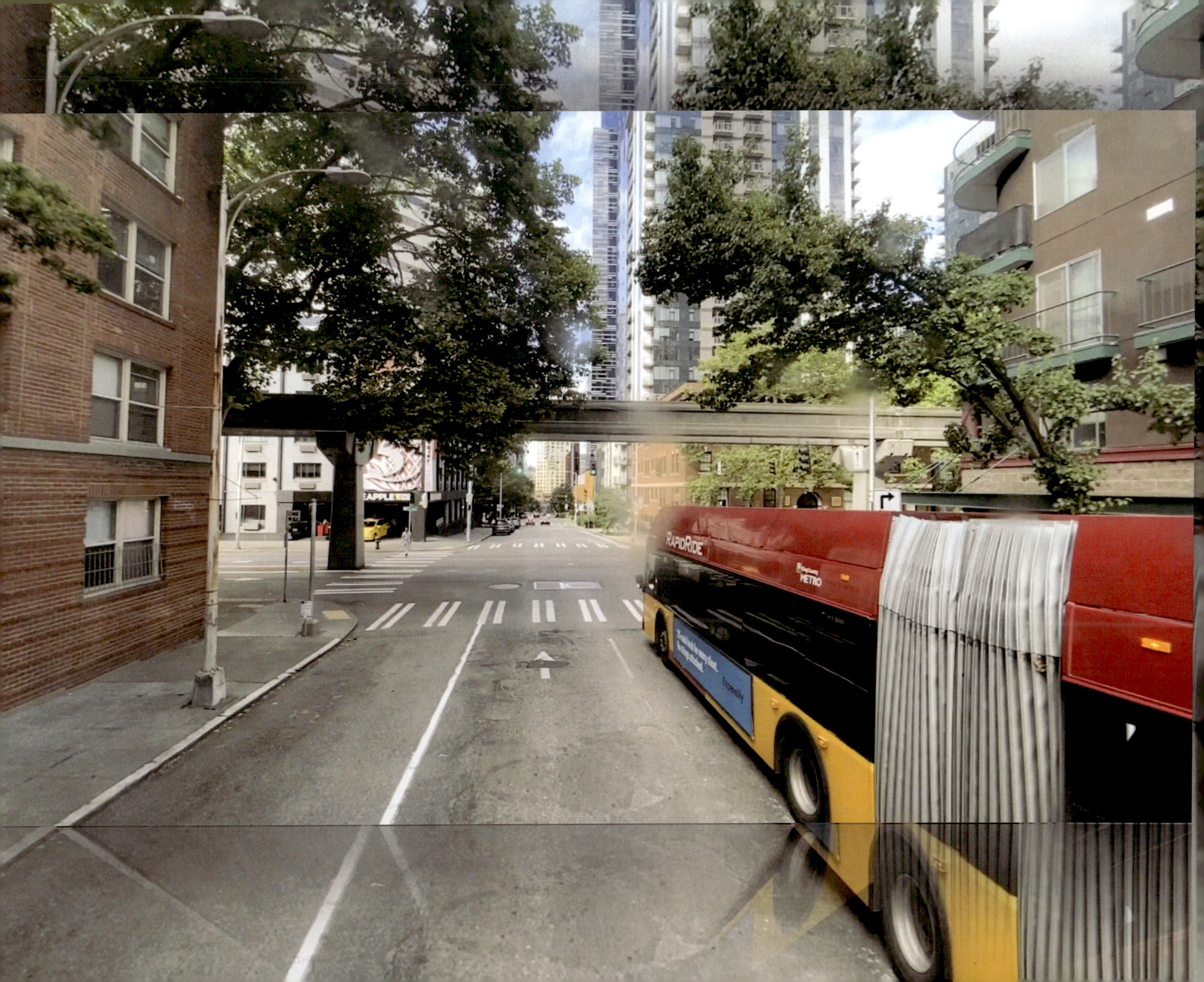
RapidRide
King County METRO

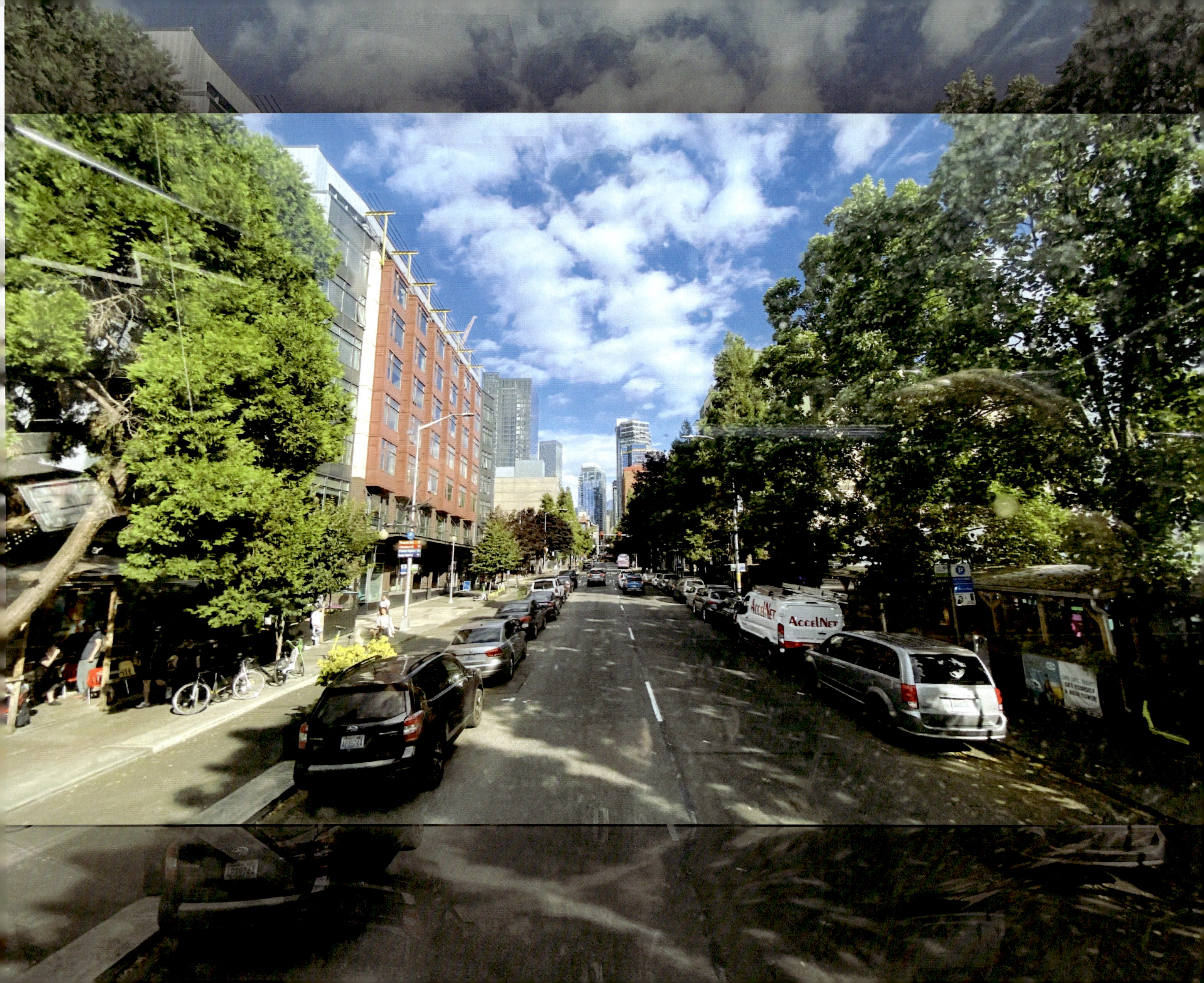

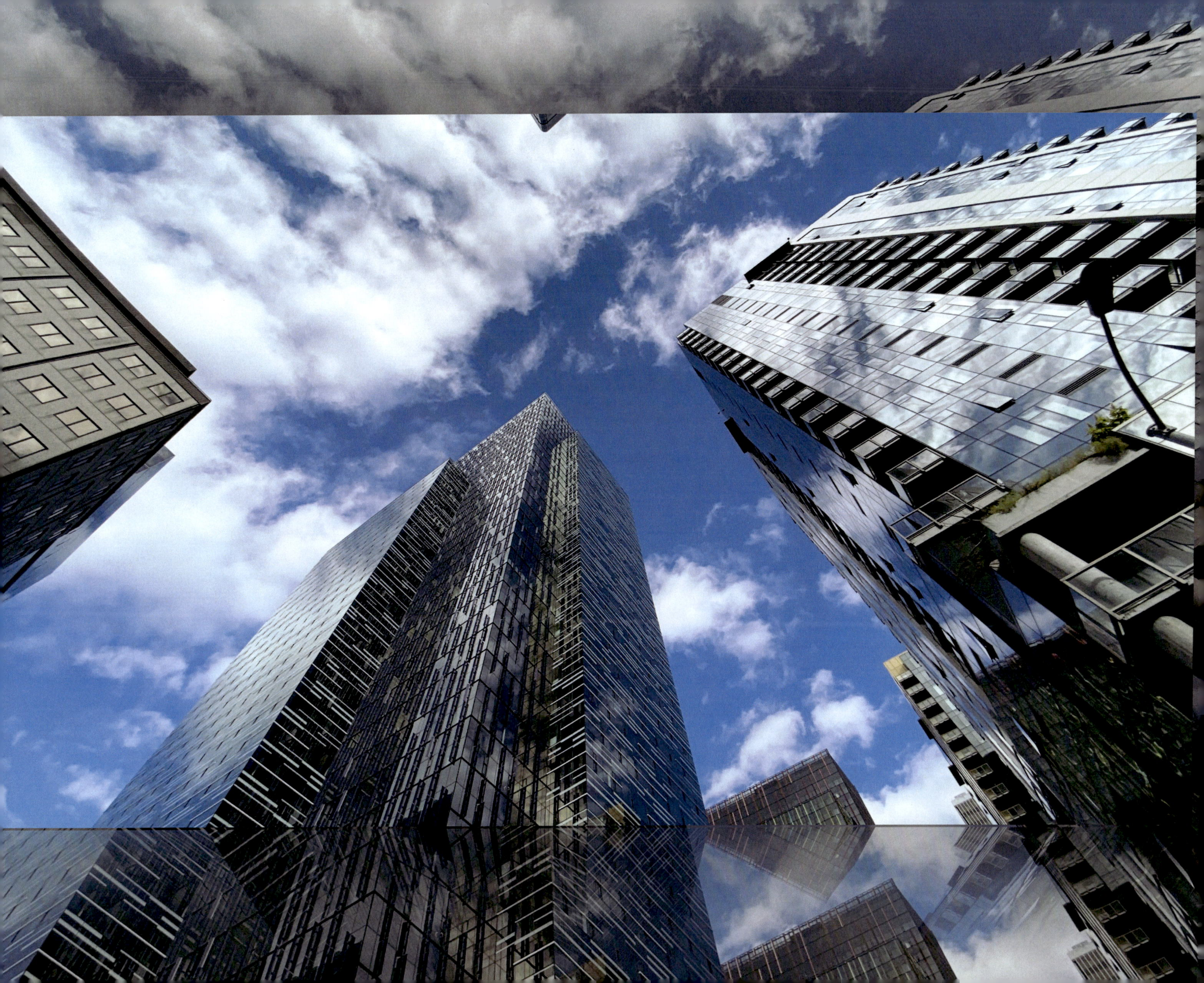

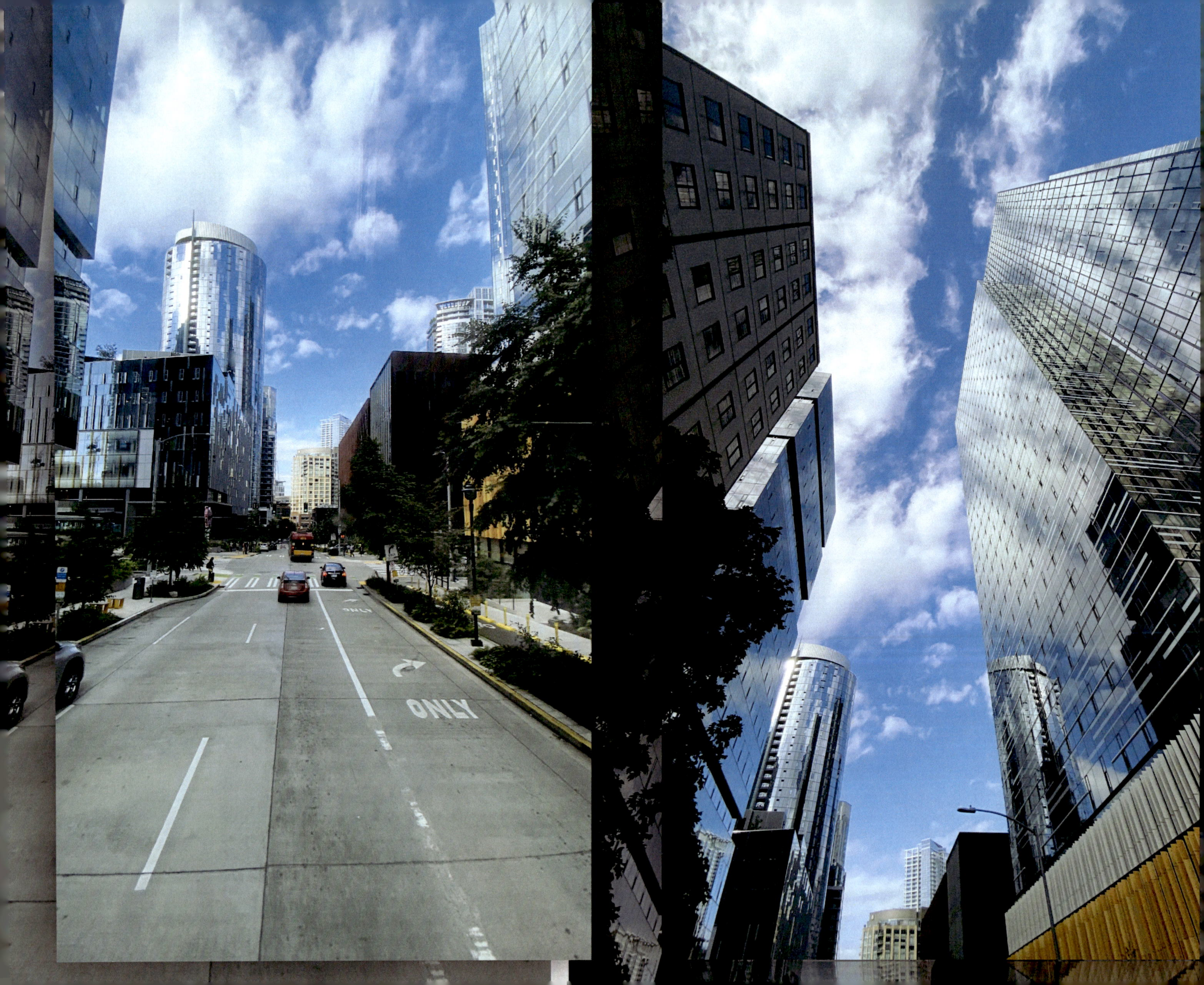

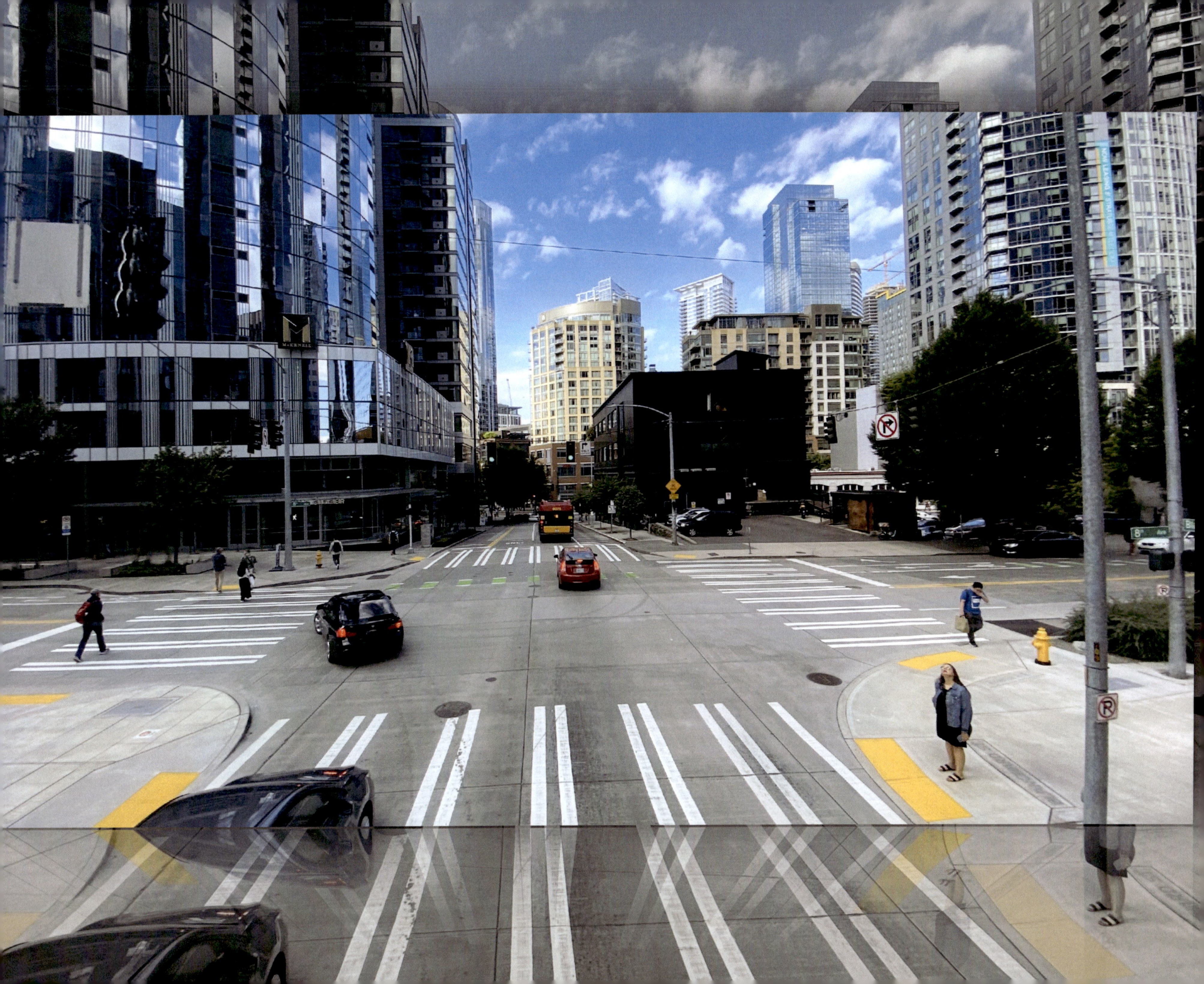

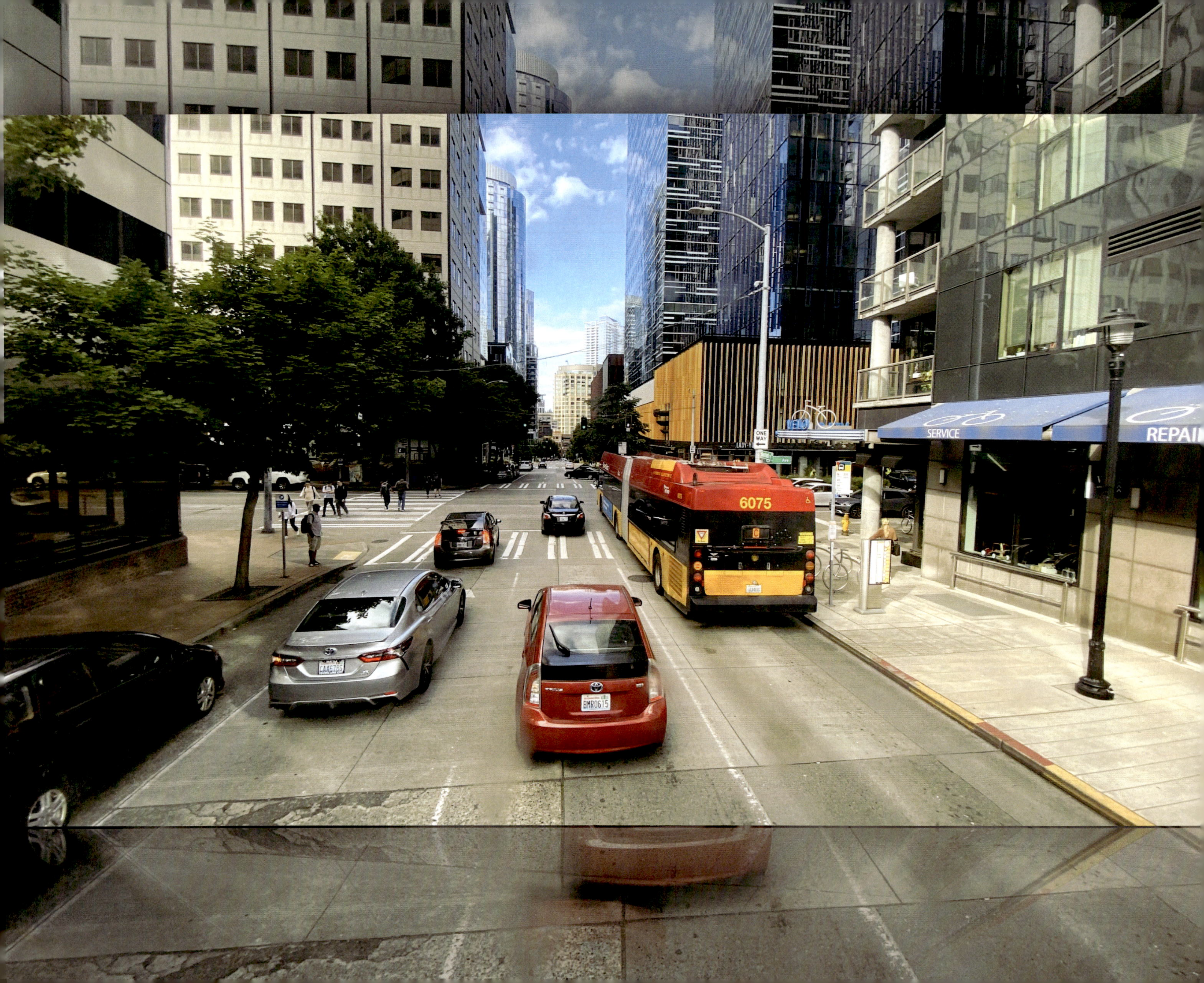
ONE WAY
SERVICE
REPAIR
VELO
6075
BMR0615

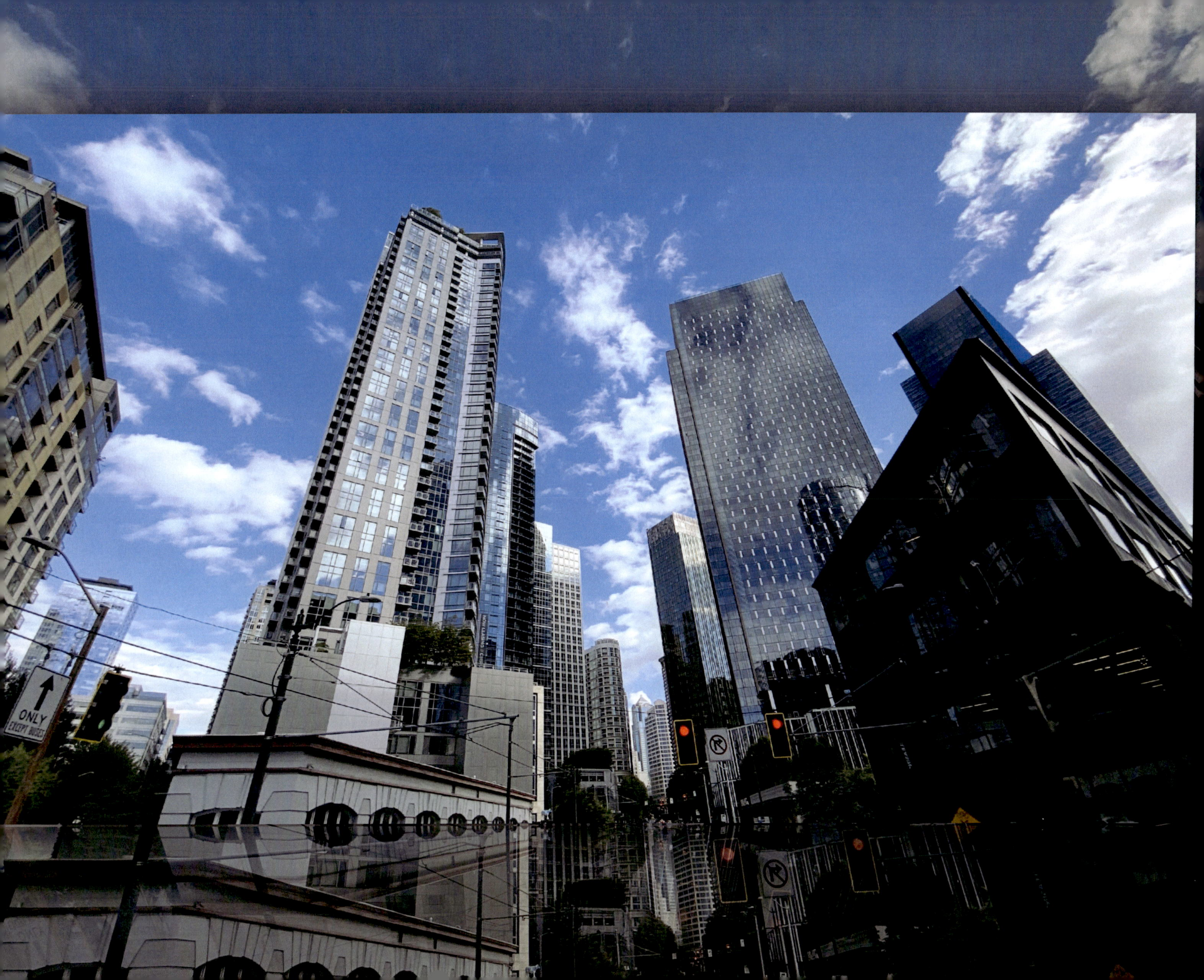
ONLY
EXCEPT BUSES

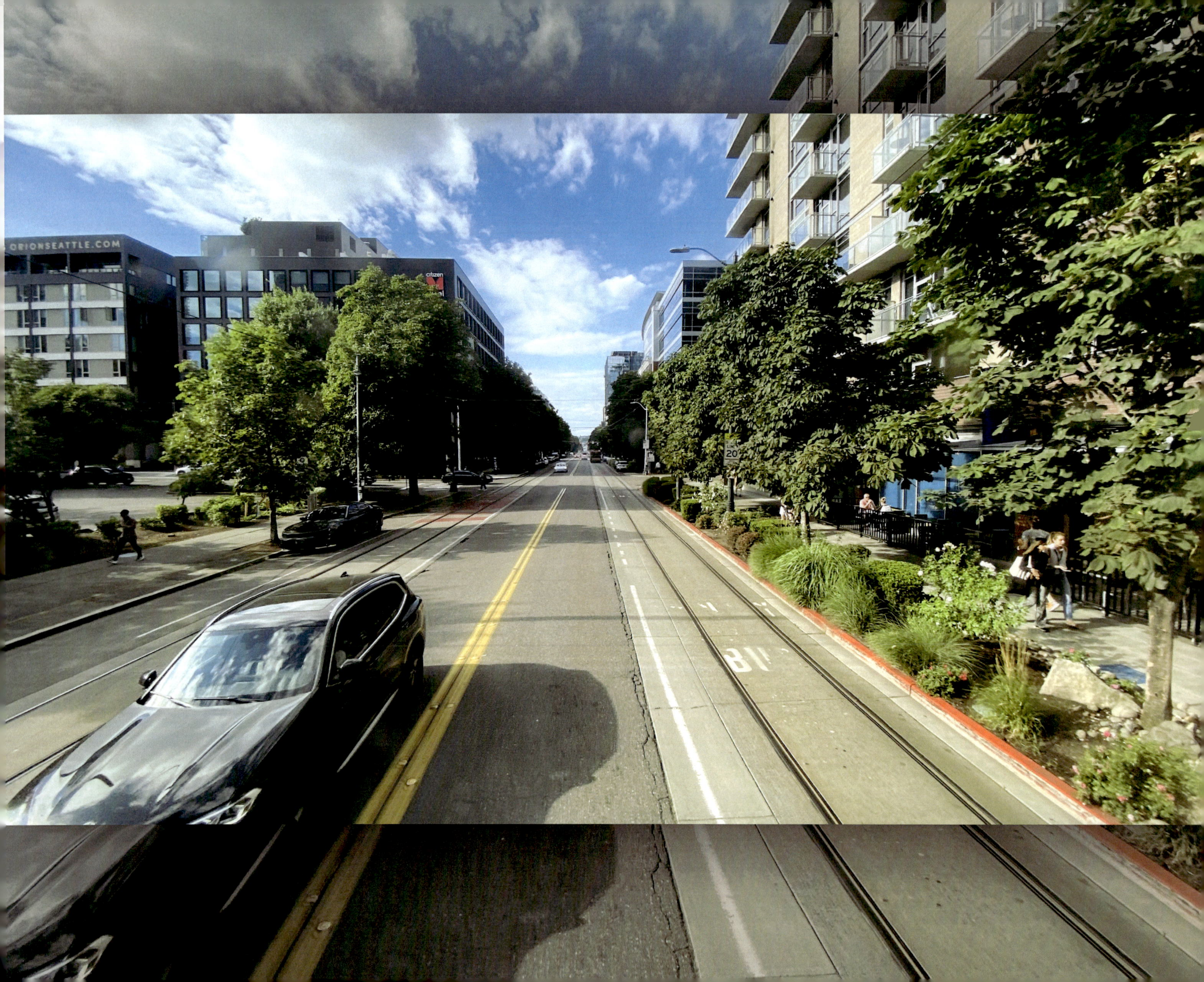
ORIONSEATTLE.COM
citizen
20

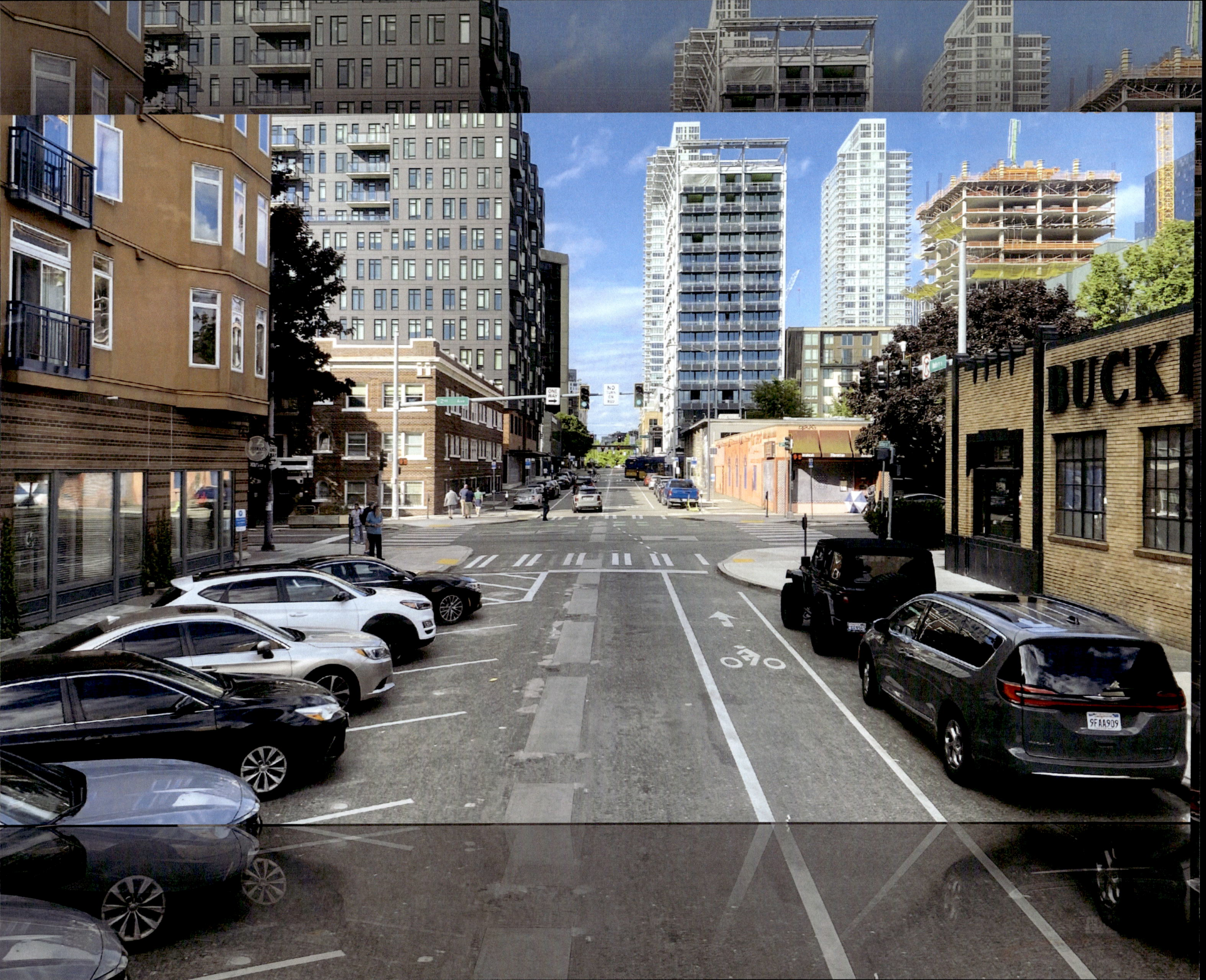
ONE
WAY
BUCK

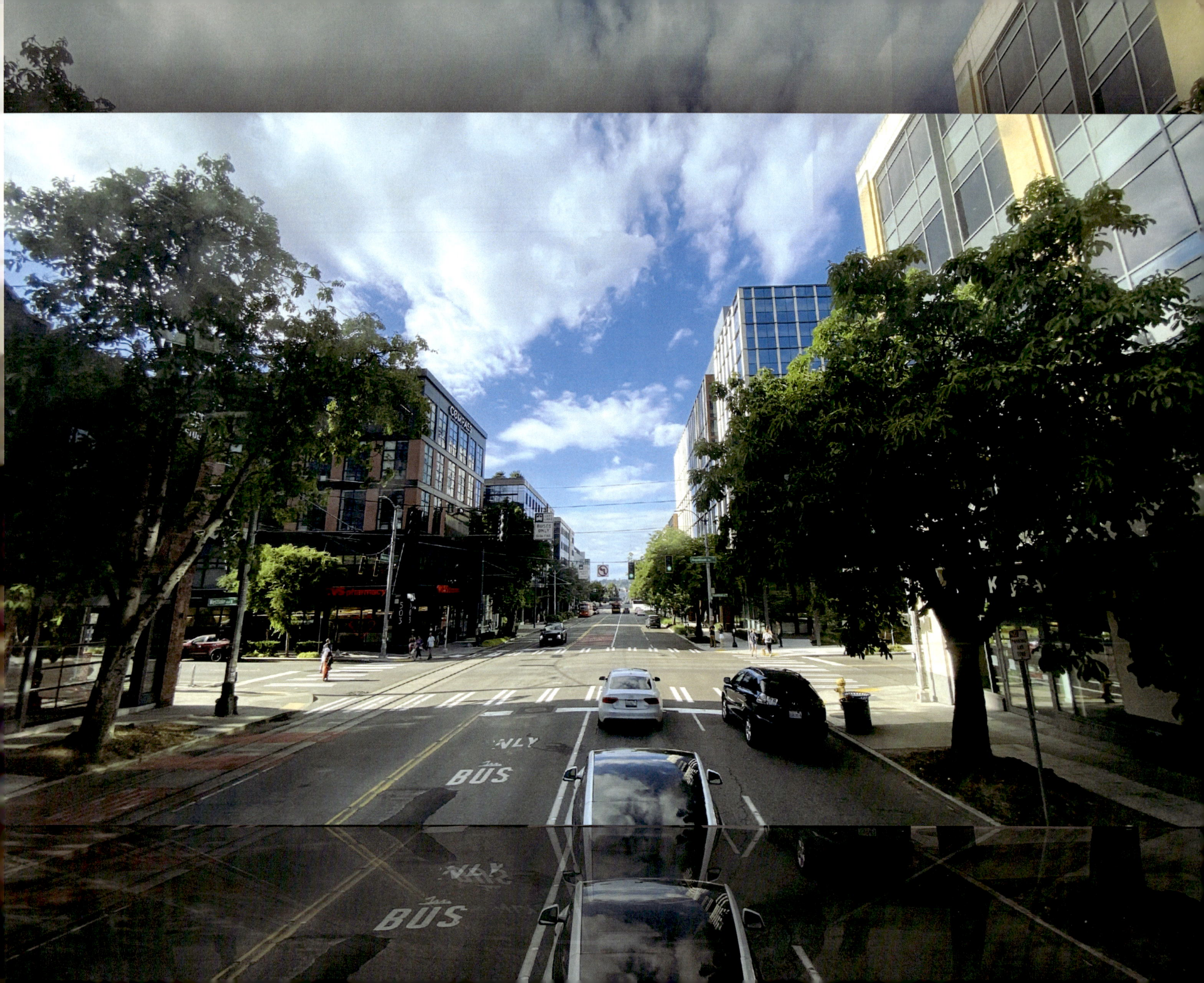

I wanted to take a moment to express my heartfelt gratitude to you. Your kindness and support have meant the world to me. Whether it was lending an ear, offering a helping hand, or simply being there, your presence has made a significant difference in my life.

Thank you for your unwavering encouragement and belief in me. Your words of wisdom have guided me through challenges and inspired me to reach new heights. I am truly fortunate to have you in my corner.

Please know that your generosity has not gone unnoticed. Your thoughtfulness has touched my heart in ways I cannot fully express. I am deeply grateful for everything you have done for me.

As we continue on our journey together, I look forward to the moments we will share and the memories we will create. Thank you for being an incredible friend, mentor, and source of light in my life.

www.ingramcontent.com/pod-product-compliance
Lightning Source LLC
Chambersburg PA
CBRC100745110726
48005CB00010B/1045